Human Capital and Development

N.S. Siddharthan • K. Narayanan
Editors

Human Capital and Development

The Indian Experience

Springer

Editors
N.S. Siddharthan
Madras School of Economics
Chennai
Tamil Nadu, India

K. Narayanan
Department of Humanities
and Social Sciences
Indian Institute of Technology Bombay
Mumbai
Maharashtra, India

ISBN 978-81-322-1717-6 ISBN 978-81-322-0857-0 (eBook)
DOI 10.1007/978-81-322-0857-0
Springer New Delhi Heidelberg New York Dordrecht London

Printed on acid-free paper

Springer is part of Springer Science+Business Media (www.springer.com)

Preface and Acknowledgements

The chapters included in this volume are revised versions of papers presented at the Fifth Annual Conference of the Forum for Global Knowledge Sharing (http://FGKS.in) (Knowledge Forum), hosted by the Department of Humanities and Social Sciences, Indian Institute of Technology Bombay (IIT B), during 11–12 November 2010. The conference was jointly held with Indian Association of Social Science Institutions (IASSI). All the papers, except the last one, were presented in the conference. The last paper was included since it addresses the issues of efficiency and the role of government in technical education in India.

Forum for Global Knowledge Sharing is a specialised, interdisciplinary, web-based global forum. It deals with science, technology and economy interface. It aims at providing a platform for scholars belonging to different institutions, universities, countries and disciplines to interact, exchange their research findings and undertake joint research studies. It is designed for persons who have been contributing to R&D and publishing their research findings in professional journals. It is mainly a web-based or a virtual forum with a registered office housed at the Institute for Human Development (IHD), New Delhi. Knowledge Forum was registered on 25 August 2005. The membership to the forum is open to all scholars who have been publishing in refereed professional journals. We have about 250 registered members belonging to different disciplines and institutions and countries. We have now more than 125 research papers in the *Research Papers* folder.

Even though it is chiefly a web-based forum, we do hold annual conferences where the members present their research papers, share research findings with other members and interact. Knowledge Forum annual international conferences have been well attended and the papers have been of a high quality.

About 60 persons registered and participated in the conference held at IIT Bombay. In addition to scholars from different Indian universities and institutions, scholars from Lancaster University, UK; UNU-MERIT, the Netherlands; Lessius University College, Antwerp, Belgium; Pardos Marketing, France; and Georgetown University, Washington, DC, USA, participated in the conference.

Chapters included in the volume were revised based on the detailed comments given by the discussants and participants from the floor of the conference. We are grateful to the discussants, Professors K. L. Krishna (Delhi School of Economics), Y. S. Rajan (ISRO), Ashok Jain (former director NISTAS), B. N. Goldar (Institute of Economic Growth), L. M. Bhole (IIT B) and V. N. Balasubramaniam (Lancaster University) for giving detailed comments and suggestions on the papers. We thank the Director, IIT Bombay and the faculty, staff and students of the Department of Humanities and Social Sciences, IIT Bombay, for hosting the seminar, providing excellent arrangements and creating a conducive atmosphere for academic discussion. We are grateful to Mr Santosh Kumar Sahu, Research Scholar, Department of Humanities and Social Sciences, IIT Bombay, for research support and assistance in preparing this manuscript. We express our thanks to all the authors for agreeing to submit their papers for publication.

Madras School of Economics, Chennai — N.S. Siddharthan
Department of Humanities and Social Sciences — K. Narayanan
IIT Bombay, Mumbai

Contents

1 **Human Capital and Development: Introduction** 1
N.S. Siddharthan and K. Narayanan

2 **Human Capital, Labour Productivity and Employment** 11
Savita Bhat and N.S. Siddharthan

3 **Impact of Human Capital on Manufacturing Productivity Growth in India** 23
Vinish Kathuria, S.N. Rajesh Raj, and Kunal Sen

4 **Informality, Vulnerability and Development** 39
Dibyendu Maiti and Arup Mitra

5 **Labour and Energy Intensity: A Study of the Pulp and Paper Industries in India** 55
Santosh Kumar Sahu and K. Narayanan

6 **Impact of Remittances on Poverty in India: Empirical Evidence** 77
Rashmi Banga and Pritish Kumar Sahu

7 **Understanding NREGA: A Simple Theory and Some Facts** 103
Diganta Mukherjee and Uday Bhanu Sinha

8 **Measuring Efficiency of Technical Education Institutions in Kerala Using Data Envelopment Analysis** 129
S. Sunitha and Malathy Duraisamy

Author Index 147

Subject Index 153

Contributors

Rashmi Banga Unit of Economic Cooperation & Integration Among Developing Countries, UNCTAD, Geneva

Savita Bhat Amrita School of Business, Bangalore, India

Malathy Duraisamy Department of Humanities and Social Sciences, Indian Institute of Technology (IIT) Madras, Chennai, India

Vinish Kathuria SJMSOM, Indian Institute of Technology Bombay, Mumbai, India

Dibyendu Maiti Institute of Economic Growth, University of Delhi Enclave, Delhi, India

Arup Mitra Institute of Economic Growth, University of Delhi Enclave, Delhi, India

Diganta Mukherjee Indian Statistical Institute, Kolkata, India

K. Narayanan Department of Humanities and Social Sciences, Indian Institute of Technology, Bombay, Powai, Mumbai, India

S.N. Rajesh Raj Centre for Multi-Disciplinary Development Research, Dharwad, India

Pritish Kumar Sahu Faculty of Business and Law, Multimedia University, Melaka, Malaysia

Santosh Kumar Sahu Department of Humanities and Social Sciences, Indian Institute of Technology, Bombay, Powai, Mumbai, India

Kunal Sen IDPM, University of Manchester, Manchester, UK

N.S. Siddharthan Madras School of Economics, Chennai, India

Uday Bhanu Sinha Department of Economics, Delhi School of Economics, University of Delhi, New Delhi, India

S. Sunitha School of Management Studies, National Institute of Technology (NIT) Calicut, Calicut, India

Chapter 1
Human Capital and Development: Introduction

N.S. Siddharthan and K. Narayanan

Given the contemporary socio-economic reality in terms of disparities in standard of living, inequity in access to resources, policy asymmetries across countries and coexistence of higher growth with poverty in developing countries, it is widely believed that there is a need for enhancement and appropriate utilisation of human skills to foster development. India and other large emerging economies have great potential for achieving high-economic growth if only they could use their demographic dividend much more judiciously. There has been a great deal of theoretical understanding and rich empirical evidence on the link between human capital and development. However, the gross enrolment ratio in both school and higher education has been a cause for concern in several developing countries. The needs of the changing pattern of industrialisation, which demands more and more skilled manpower, are also going unmatched by the supply. What are the paradigms available in the context of modern development? How appropriate could they be specifically for India? How can one evaluate the suitability of different paradigms? What are the interlinkages between skill content of the workforce and competitiveness of industries? These are some of the questions that we have addressed in this volume.

N.S. Siddharthan (✉)
Madras School of Economics, Chennai, India
e-mail: nssiddharthan@gmail.com

K. Narayanan
Department of Humanities and Social Sciences, Indian Institute of Technology Bombay, Powai, Mumbai, India
e-mail: knn@iitb.ac.in

N.S. Siddharthan and K. Narayanan (eds.), *Human Capital and Development: The Indian Experience*, DOI 10.1007/978-81-322-0857-0_1, © Springer India 2013

1.1 Human Capital and Economic Development

The issues relating to the role of human capital in fostering economic growth and development of an economy have been of interest to several economists. In the traditional neoclassical growth models by Solow and Swan in 1950s, the output of an economy grows in response to larger inputs of capital and labour. Furthermore, the economy under these models conforms to the "law of diminishing returns to scale". With these assumptions, the neoclassical growth models analyse some implications to the economy; in particular, they show that as the capital stock increases, growth of the economy slows down, and in order to keep the economy growing, it must capitalise from incessant infusions of technological progress. It is well known that this mechanism in neoclassical growth model is neither inherent nor does it strive to explain much; this simply means that the technological progress is "exogenous" to the system. Addressing the above issues, in the mid-1980s, a new paradigm was developed in the literature, mostly due to the Romer (1986), which is now commonly known as "endogenous growth models". In simple terms, what this means is that if the firm which invests in capital also employs educated and skilled workers who are also healthy, then not only will the labour be more productive but will also be able to use the capital and technology more efficiently. This will lead to a "Hicks neutral" shift in the production function, and thus there can be "increasing" rather than "decreasing" returns to investments. In other words, technology and human capital are both "endogenous" to the system. The theoretical models of economic growth have underscored the role of human capital. The empirical analysis of growth for a broad group of countries shows that the school attainment has positive effect on growth (Barro 1992). Many studies have found that a region's growth is influenced by the initial level of human capital. Glaeser et al. (1995) find that human capital level in 1960 influences growth of the cities between 1960 and 1990. Similarly, Simon and Nardinelli (2002) found that cities that have higher level of human capital grow faster in the long run.

Few factors are as important in raising labour productivity as human capital investments. While the average years of schooling in many Asian countries have increased substantially during the last few decades, this has not necessarily led to the workers having the skills and training that help them obtain higher quality employment. Moreover, low level of human capital may be a constraint to investment and expansion in sectors that require skilled workers. As markets in countries at different stages of development typically demand different skill sets, educational investments and policy are likely to vary with these needs. In particular, low-income countries with a high proportion of informal workers may need to consider developing a focused and narrow set of skills through vocational education and training programmes. However, middle-income countries that are trying to move up the value chain may require more general tertiary education that allows for the development of innovative ideas. As Foster (2011) noted, the informal labour market in agriculture that exists in many low-income countries may reflect the shifting nature of agricultural labour demand; it may also indicate lack of specialisation in particular land or tasks. By contrast, most self-employed workers and most factory workers outside of the farm sector may have specific skills that cannot easily be replaced by someone working in another sector. Thus, the rents associated with these skills should appear in terms of labour market earnings. Because specific skills are associated with nonfarm employment, a wage premium is observed for many forms of nonfarm employment (Lanjouw and Murgai 2008), which suggests focusing on training and educational programmes that can allow nonfarm workers in rural areas to develop a specific set of skills.

Entrepreneurship training is also a potentially useful tool for raising the income of micro-entrepreneurs. Karlan and Valdivia (2006) used a randomised treatment that added business training to an existing micro-credit programme in Peru to study the impacts of entrepreneurial training. They found that the training increased repayment and business revenues for the clients. This provided evidence that important management skills can be taught. While the pendulum has swung from an emphasis on technical and vocational education and training (TVET) programmes in the 1980s and early 1990s to an emphasis on general education programmes since the mid-1990s, there is limited research to firmly resolve the debate on which type of education is more beneficial. Because students who enrol in TVET may have, overall, different backgrounds and educational competencies from those who elect general education, it has usually been impossible to assess which track of education may be better.

Horowitz and Schenzler (1999), correcting for selection bias, found that general education exceeded returns to TVET in Suriname. Conversely, Malamud and Pop-Eleches (2008), using an education reform that shifted a large proportion of students from vocational training to general education while keeping the average years of schooling unchanged, found that in Romania there were no differences in returns between graduates of vocational versus those of general schools. However, the difference in findings may reflect the quality of the general education versus the technical vocational education institutions. In general, expanding and strengthening vocational education opportunities can serve an important purpose, especially in a rapidly growing, liberalised economy. Vocational education can also be a powerful tool for improving job prospects and job quality among the poor. For example, in Vietnam, which still has a large agricultural sector, people with vocational education were shown to have greater success in finding employment and higher wages than people with general education up to the secondary level, but had slightly lower employment and earnings than people who had general tertiary education. Ultimately, as economies evolve and become more service oriented, promoting TVET may no longer be very useful for the majority of the population.

Newhouse and Suryadarma (2011) examined the labour market outcomes of Indonesian youths who entered the TVET track and those who entered the general education track for senior high school. They found that female TVET graduates were able to get more jobs and higher wages than males who had general education. They cited concerns over expanding public vocational education and the relevance of the skills taught by TVET, especially for males in an increasingly service-oriented economy. In general, there is a strong role for building human capital to improve employment outcomes, whether through vocational or general education. Both systems and institutions may need to be strengthened. For workers in developing countries who are largely going to become self-employed, having a very specific skill to market seems warranted. However, as countries upscale and evolve, it may be preferable to focus more on general education, which may better impart the flexibility and innovation that is useful for service-oriented economies.

1.2 Technology, FDI and Skill Intensity

Several studies have shown that current technology favours the use of skilled labour force (Salvanes and Forre 2003; Kim 1998) and production of differentiated products (Kim 1998). The world market is growing mainly in high-tech and skill-intensive goods. The global market for standardised goods is either stagnating or declining (Lall 1999). Under these conditions industrial units using skill-intensive workforce and producing differentiated and high-quality products are likely to grow faster and thereby contribute to growth and employment. Furthermore, some other studies have documented (Ciccone and Papaioannou 2009) that countries with higher education levels experienced faster value addition and employment growth. In the context of the industrial sector, some studies argue and show that the ownership pattern of industries could make a difference. For example, a study for Turkey (Alvan and Ghosh 2010) shows that human capital's contribution to growth was mainly confined to the private sector and not to the public sector. By and large, there is general agreement that the current technology is mainly knowledge and skill intensive, and the quality of human capital plays an important role in the growth of industries, agriculture and services sectors.

The layout and the format of the information technology using factories are very different from the traditional factories. The new factories are characterised by flexible manufacturing practices, multi-skilled workforce, flexible job responsibilities, few managerial layers, better inventory management and increased outsourcing activities in contrast to the earlier ones that had almost the opposite characteristics (Brynjolfsson and Hitt 2000).

There is also evidence to show that human capital in host countries has also been influencing the inflow of foreign direct investments (FDI). For example, the study by Noorbakhsh et al. (2001) shows that despite a dramatic increase in FDI inflows to developing countries, only a few countries have been receiving FDI and the host countries could improve their location advantage by investing in human capital and increasing the skill content of their workforce. Furthermore, the US FDI outflows have also been attracted by country skill-labour abundance and industry skill intensities (Yeaple 2003). There is also evidence to show that regional/state governments within a country that have been spending more on human resources have been attracting more FDI (for interstate differences in FDI inflows for India and China, see Siddharthan 2009, and for China see Broadman and Sun 1997; Wei 1999). FDI inflows could also contribute to skill development in the host countries (Doctor 2007).

Even in traditional areas like agriculture skill-intensive operations are on the increase. Thus, the link between human resource development and economic development has also got strengthened. This emerging phenomenon has resulted in a scarcity of skilled and educated workforce and a huge backlog of unemployed persons who are not sufficiently skilled. To create employment for this unskilled workforce, it has become vital for the governments to spend heavily on education at all levels – primary, secondary and university (including technical education).

Scholars from different disciplines in economics and other social sciences have been working in these areas. Though the issues involved cut across disciplines and so require a multidisciplinary approach involving interaction between scholars from different disciplines, there is no forum or platform to facilitate scholars belonging to science, technology, business schools, economics and other social sciences to come together to present their research findings in one volume. This book is in response to this vital need. So far, there is no comprehensive volume that addresses these issues as systematically as we have done in this book.

The theme "Human Capital and Development" has several dimensions, and the chapters included in the volume cover several dimensions and discuss the following aspects:

- Knowledge revolution and the changing role of skilled workforce
- Skill-biased technological change and job destruction of low-skilled workers
- Human resource, labour productivity and employment
- Foreign direct investment and human resources
- Human capital, energy use and environment
- Human capital and antipoverty programmes
- Government and efficiency of educational institutions

1.3 Guided Tour of the Chapters

Several studies argue that the current technology is human capital and knowledge intensive and cannot be used in the absence of investment in skill development. Quite a few studies also emphasise the skill bias in the technology. The first two chapters in this volume test for the role of skill differences among the Indian states in influencing productivity, its growth and employment. In Chap. 2, Bhat and Siddharthan hypothesise a positive relationship between skill content of the population and labour productivity and growth of labour productivity and employment. The chapter measures interstate skill differentials through enrolment rates in middle and high schools. Using a balanced panel for 21 Indian states for the period 2003–2007, they showed that after controlling for fixed capital and other control variables, human capital as represented by higher education levels and health infrastructure come out significant in influencing interstate differences in labour productivity, its growth and growth of employment. In addition, states that enjoyed higher levels of urbanisation and industrial agglomeration experienced higher levels of labour productivity and employment growth. The chapter advocates emphasis on education and health facilities to achieve productivity and employment growths.

The next chapter (Chap. 3) by Kathuria, Raj and Sen analyse the role of human capital in influencing total factor productivity in the Indian manufacturing sectors. They also examine interstate differences. However, they use enterprise level data to investigate whether differences in the total factor productivity growth for the same industries across 15 major Indian states covering both formal and informal sectors are influenced by human capital differences. They consider 90 industries for the periods 1994–1995 and 2005–2006. They find human capital (literacy rate) important for productivity growth only for the formal sector. Furthermore, total factor productivity steadily grew only in the formal sector. In fact it recorded a negative growth rate for the informal sector. The chapter not only emphasises the role of human capital in influencing growth of productivity but also the importance of the formal manufacturing sector. Export and import intensities did not influence productivities in the manufacturing sector across the states.

The finding of negative growth rate of productivity of the informal sector leads to the question of gainful employment in the informal sector. The more general question relates to the access of the Indian workforce to productive employment. This question is important for India as the growth is taking place accompanied by informalisation. In this context it is important to find out whether acquisition of skills enables workers in the informal sector to graduate and move to the formal sector. Furthermore, does informalisation accentuate inequalities? The chapter (Chap. 4) by Maiti and Mitra addresses some of these important questions. As in the case of the earlier two chapters, this chapter also deals with interstate differences. It estimates the size of the informal sector in nonfarm employment. In particular, it derives the index of informal sector employment that could be attributed to the distress led or supply pushed phenomenon. The results show that development expenditure aimed at improving education, health and infrastructure facilities, results in a decline in distress led informalisation. These very same variables explained labour productivity and employment growth (Chap. 2). Thus, the three chapters taken together convey an important and consistent message.

The next chapter (Chap. 5) deals with another important issue relating to human capital, namely, the relationship between labour intensity and energy savings. For this purpose it takes the Indian paper and pulp industry as a case study. This industry is one of the most energy and pollution intensive industries, and if it could be shown that labour input and energy input are substitutes, then energy consumption could be reduced by employing more of skilled labour. The results of the study by Narayanan and Sahu show that labour and energy intensity has an inverted U shape relationship, suggesting a substitution possibility between energy and labour for the pulp and paper industries in India. Furthermore, the results also showed a negative relationship between energy intensity and technology intensity. Thus, by spending more on labour and technology, the units could significantly bring down energy intensity. In this chapter labour intensity is measured by the sum spent on labour as a proportion of sales turnover. This definition takes into account the skill content of the workforce. Higher proportion spent on labour could indicate employment of better skilled workers as the wage rate for low-skilled workers are very low.

The next chapter (Chap. 6) by Banga and Sahu deals with another important aspect of human capital, namely, the migration of workers and the remittances repatriated back to India. India is one of the highest recipients of remittances in the world. The study analyses the impact of remittances on poverty in India. Among all the Indian states, Kerala has the highest percentage of non-resident Indians. Hence, the study gives special emphasis on Kerala. There are very few studies on the export of human capital, remittances and its impact on poverty and development. This study fills this major gap in literature. Banga and Sahu argue that unlike other financial flows, remittances are more stable and predictable, and what is more they could also provide a cushion against economic shocks. The study also indicates remittances and other variables like poverty and state per capita income could have two-way relationships. Nevertheless, it does have an influence in reducing poverty. Furthermore, estimates for Kerala show a definite impact of remittances on per capita income and investments.

The discussion on remittances and poverty leads to an analysis of other measures aimed at reducing poverty. In Chap. 7, Mukherjee and Sinha examine one of the most important antipoverty programmes, namely, the National Rural Employment Guarantee Act (NREGA). The chapter develops a theoretical model to analyse the impact of NREGA on rural labour market, income of the poor households and agricultural production. One of the predictions of the model is that consequent to the introduction of NREGA, the cultivating households will employ less labour thereby adversely affecting production. There is some evidence to support this prediction. However, the poor would be better off. Their model also predicts increases in food prices due to the introduction of NREGA.

The last chapter (Chap. 8) deals with a very different aspect of human capital, namely, efficiency of education institutions. Sunita and Duraisamy, using the data envelopment analysis, evaluate the efficiency of engineering colleges and technical institutes of Kerala. They use the number of teaching, nonteaching and nonpersonnel expenditures as inputs and student enrolment as output. They found the government institutions more technical and scale efficient than the private institutions. This finding reinforces the crucial role of government in promoting higher education. The private sector could at best complement the government. In other words, the government cannot withdraw from higher education and leave the field to the private sector.

The chapters included in this volume cover several aspects of human capital. It starts with the role of human capital in influencing productivity, employment and growth of employment. The chapters show that Indian states that have been neglecting schooling and health facilities have become victims in terms of low productivity and lower rates of employment. Consequently, employment cannot be increased without spending on education and health. Furthermore, the unorganised sector in India cannot provide gainful employment as productivity in this sector is low and is also declining. Skill-intensity influences mainly productivity in the organised sector. As a result, states that have been neglecting human capital would lose on both counts.

The chapters also reveal that human capital could be substituted for energy use and help in reducing energy consumption and pollution. India is also one of the important exporters of human capital, and the non-resident Indians send remittances back to India. The volume indicates that remittances play a significant role in poverty reduction and increase in per capita consumption levels. In addition remittances, unlike foreign direct investments and portfolio investments, are less erratic and are not influenced by slowdown in the world economy. Poverty could also be directly attacked through the use of antipoverty programmes like NREGA. This volume provides an analytical framework and a theoretical model to analyse the impact of these programmes to examine their influence on labour demand, income, prices and productivity. The volume also emphasises the crucial role of the government in directly running education institutions. As seen from the volume, government run engineering institutions are technically more efficient than the private run ones.

In sum, the theme *Human Capital and Development* has several dimensions. This volume tries to cover as many aspects as possible. It has chapters dealing with the following features: skill bias of the current technology and its consequences for growth and employment; negative implications of skill bias on the unorganised sector and an analysis of remedial measures like antipoverty programmes and in particular NREGA; the role of remittances as a consequence of migration of human capital in poverty alleviation and economic development; role of government in improving skill content of the population by directly funding education institutions, including investment in technical education; and importance of human capital in energy conservation in manufacturing skilled labour as a substitute for energy.

References

Alvan A, Ghosh BN (2010) Productivity and growth in Turkish manufacturing industry: 1980–2001. J Develop Areas 43(2):187–219

Barro RJ (1992) Human capital and economic growth. In: Proceedings of Federal Reserve Bank of Kansas City, pp 199–230

Broadman HG, Sun X (1997) The distribution of foreign direct investment in China. World Econ 20(3):339–361

Brynjolfsson E, Hitt LM (2000) Beyond computation: information technology, organizational transformation and business performance. J Econ Perspect 14(4):23–48

Ciccone A, Papaioannou E (2009) Human capital structure of production and growth. Rev Econ Stat 91(1):66–82

Doctor M (2007) Boosting investment and growth: the role of social pacts in the Brazilian automotive industry. Oxf Dev Stud 35(1):105–30

Foster AD (2011) Creating Good Employment Opportunities for the Rural Sector. Asian Development Bank Economics working paper series no. 271, http://dx.doi.org/10.2139/ssrn.1940166

Glaeser E, Scheinkman J, Shleifer A (1995) Economic growth in a cross-section of cities. J Monet Econ 36:117–143

Horowitz A, Schenzler C (1999) Returns to general, technical and vocational education in developing countries: recent evidence from Suriname. Educ Econ 7(1):5–20

Karlan D, Valdivia M (2006) Teaching entrepreneurship: impact of business training on microfinance clients and institutions. Yale University, Mimeo

Kim KS (1998) Global integration, capital and labor: a north–south comparative perspective. In: Dabir-Alai P, Odekon M (eds) Economic liberalization and labor markets. Greenwood Press, Westport, pp 25–44

Lall S (1999) India's manufactured exports: comparative structure and prospects. World Dev 27(10):1769–1786

Lanjouw P, Murgai R (2008) Poverty decline, agricultural wages and non-farm employment in rural India: 1983–2004. Working paper no. 437, Stanford University

Malamud O, Pop-Eleches C (2008) General education vs. vocational training: evidence from an economy in transition. Working paper no. 0807, University of Chicago

Newhouse D, Suryadarma D (2011) The value of vocational education: high school type and labor market outcomes in Indonesia. World Bank Econ Rev 25(2):296–322

Noorbakhsh F, Paloni A, Youssef A (2001) Human capital and FDI inflows to developing countries: new empirical evidence. World Dev 29(9):1593–1610

Romer PM (1986) Increasing returns and long-run growth, the journal of political economy, 94 (5) 1002–1037

Salvanes KG, Forre ES (2003) Effects on employment of trade and technical change: evidence from Norway. Economica 70:293–329

Siddharthan NS (2009) FDI, determinants, constraints and impact: India–China comparison. In: Agarwal M (ed) India's economic future. Social Science Press, New Delhi, pp 71–102

Simon CJ, Nardinelli C (2002) Human capital and the rise of American cities, 1900–1990. Reg Sci Urban Econ 32:59–96

Wei Y (1999) The regional distribution of foreign direct investment in China. Reg Stud 33(9):857–67

Yeaple SR (2003) The role of skill endowments in the structure of US outward FDI. Rev Econ Stat 85(3):726–34

Chapter 2
Human Capital, Labour Productivity and Employment

Savita Bhat and N.S. Siddharthan

2.1 Introduction

This chapter analyses the crucial role played by human capital in determining the interstate differences in labour productivity and its growth in India. In addition, the chapter deals with the impact of human capital differences on the growth of employment for a cross section of Indian states for the period 2003–2007. Labour productivity has been taken up for analysis, as sustained growth of per capita income is not possible without growth in labour productivity. It can be shown that per capita income is a product of labour productivity and the share of labour force in population.[1] Since the share of labour force in population cannot be altered in the short and medium runs, per capita income cannot increase without an increase in labour productivity. Furthermore, due to the presence of decreasing returns to scale, sustained growth of income is not possible merely by increasing investments in capital stock.

It is, therefore, argued that for sustained growth of per capita income, investment has to be accompanied by technological change. Hence, studies emphasise the crucial role of technology and innovations in promoting growth (Grossman and Helpman 1991; Mankiw et al. 1992; Romer 1994; Helpman 1998). In this context, it is important to note that the current technology, which is human capital and

[1] If Y = income of the state, POP = total population of the state, and LAB = workforce of the state, then one can write $Y/\text{POP} = Y/\text{LAB} \times \text{LAB}/\text{POP}$ where Y/POP is per capita income; Y/LAB is labour productivity and LAB/POP is proportion of workers in total population.

S. Bhat
Amrita School of Business, Bangalore, India
e-mail: savitapbhat@gmail.com

N.S. Siddharthan (✉)
Madras School of Economics, Chennai, India
e-mail: nssiddharthan@gmail.com

N.S. Siddharthan and K. Narayanan (eds.), *Human Capital and Development: The Indian Experience*, DOI 10.1007/978-81-322-0857-0_2, © Springer India 2013

knowledge intensive, cannot be used in the absence of skill development. Several studies show presence of skill bias in the new technology and argue that persons with less education would remain unemployed (Salvanes and Forre 2003). Feliciano (2001) found increased wage inequalities in Mexico due to new technology and liberalisation of the economy. For the Latin American countries, in general, Kim (1998) found that the inflow of investments consequent to liberalisation created jobs mainly for skilled labour. For India, Pandit and Siddharthan (2008) showed that employment increased mainly in skill and technology-intensive industries.

2.2 Skill-Biased Development

The current technological revolution based on knowledge-based information and communications technology (ICT) is not confined to a particular sector but cuts across virtually all sectors and industries. It is more of a technological fusion. This characteristic of the ICT technology has introduced a skill bias across industries and nations. Several studies show that the current technology is more skewed towards more educated workers and the less educated workers could become victims of the new technology. For Korea, Jung and Choi (2006) show skill bias in the use of ICT and consequent structural shift resulting in a higher demand for highly skilled and high-paid jobs, thereby widening the gap in employment opportunities. This result has been further confirmed for Brazilian and Indian firms by Harrison (2008). His results based on firm-level econometric evidence suggest that for Brazil and India, new developments in ICT are diffusing rapidly across manufacturing sectors resulting in enhanced demand for skilled workers.

There are several ways of measuring skill content of the workforce. One measure that has turned important in analysing skill bias has been the percentage of workers who have completed high school education. In the absence of direct information on skill formation in India, Maiti and Mitra (2010) have considered education, specifically, enrolment ratio in engineering and management studies, as a proxy for available skill formation. They argue that with higher levels of education, the quality of labour, and thereby their employability in the formal sector of the economy, would be enhanced. Ciccone and Papaioannou (2009) document higher growth rate in schooling-intensive industries. To successfully participate in the current revolution, it is essential to have significant proportion of the workforce trained to at least high school level. Furthermore, there is evidence to show that international trade, and even trade between identical countries, can raise the relative demand for skilled labour (Epifani and Gancia 2008). By and large, countries with higher endowments of skilled labour will benefit from the current technological scene.

There is also evidence to show that trade and investment liberalisations undertaken by countries to integrate themselves with the global economy could also increase the skill bias. Several studies reveal that human capital is a statistically significant determinant of foreign direct investment (FDI) flows. Furthermore, its importance has been increasing over time (Noorbakhsh et al. 2001). The interindustry and country determinants of the US outward FDI flows are also influenced by the skilled labour abundance of the host country and industries (Yeaple 2003). For ASEAN countries, there is evidence that human resource competitiveness influences FDI inflows to various countries (Yussof and Ismail 2002). Even within a country, labour quality could influence inter-province distribution of FDI. Gao (2005) illustrates evidence from Chinese provinces. Furthermore, FDI could also contribute to the skill intensity in countries that already have reasonable skill endowments (Doctor 2007). Thus, FDI not only goes to countries and regions that have high skilled workforce, it also helps in the further improvement of the skill content of the workforce.

In sum, evidence from earlier studies suggests human capital positively influences productivity, growth, employment and FDI. This relationship is mainly attributed to the skill bias in the use of ICT, which is extensively used in most of the sectors and countries. In this chapter, we hypothesise a positive relationship between the skill content of the workforce and labour productivity, growth of productivity and employment. We measure interstate differences in skill intensity through the schooling environment prevalent in the state, namely, percentage of the population attending schools in the age group of 14–18 years. We argue that this ratio is an indicator of the importance given by the state government to human capital development and supply of educated workforce to industry. States that have been emphasising secondary and higher education will also experience higher levels of labour productivity, higher growth of labour productivity and higher growth of employment. Indian states that have been neglecting high school education will become victims of the current technological revolution and will not only experience lower productivity levels but also lower growth rates in employment, as employment opportunities for less than high school educated persons are limited.

Two measures are used to indicate labour productivity:

1. Value added divided by the number of workers employed. This measure is used by several studies, and we also use this definition. However, this measure has several limitations. Workers differ significantly and consequently differ in their emoluments. It is important to take into account the heterogeneity of workforce in the current context. To overcome this limitation of the first measure of labour productivity, some studies have used another indicator (Caves 1992; Ray 2004; Siddharthan and Lal 2004).
2. Value added per unit cost of labour, that is, value added by the amount spent on labour. This measure is the inverse of efficiency wage. It is argued that firms should be more interested in the productivity of the amounts they spend on labour rather than on an indirect measure of productivity of a representative person they have been employing.

In this chapter, both the measures have been employed. However, the results do not differ much when either of the two measures is employed.

2.3 The Model and the Determinants of Productivity

The model used in this chapter follows the standard production function approach, where

$$VA = f\,(L,C,Z) \tag{2.i}$$

VA is value added, *L* is labour, *C* is capital and *Z* denotes other variables influencing value added (output). Since the dependent variable in this chapter is labour productivity, *L* is brought to the left-hand side and labour productivity; VA/*L*, is expressed as a function of choice of technology as represented by fixed capital-labour ratio (FCL) and other variables that affect labour productivity.[2]

$$\frac{VA}{L} = F\left(\frac{C}{L}, W\right) \tag{2.ii}$$

The other variables (*W*) include environmental differences among states relating to human capital. Thus, in addition to capital intensity, state-level differences in milieu relating to human capital, presence of foreign direct investments, export orientation, industrialisation and urbanisation will also influence labour productivity. The state-level background settings are denoted by:

1. Skill measured by proportion of the age group of 14–18 years attending schools (EDU14–18)
2. Infant mortality rate (IMR)
3. Foreign direct investment to fixed capital ratio (FDI-FC)
4. Share of industries in the state domestic product (ISHARE)
5. Share of urban population to total population (URBTOT)
6. Ratio of exports to state domestic product (X-INT)

The first two variables are used to indicate the quality of labour force in the state. States with a higher proportion of the population (in the respective age groups) attending high schools are likely to be endowed with better skilled workforce compared to states with poor attendance in schools. Likewise, infant mortality rate captures the general level of health, nutrition and wellbeing of the population in the state. Low infant mortality rate would indicate better nutrition, health facilities and hygiene. Workforce from states with better nutrition and health facilities is likely to be of a better quality. Life expectancy could also indicate better health and nutrition among the workforce, but annual time series for this variable is not available for all the states; hence, this could not be used.

The literature on FDI productivity spillovers is very rich, and several studies show a positive relationship between FDI and labour productivity (Kathuria 2002; Liu 2008). Hence, in this chapter, the share of FDI in fixed capital is used to denote the

[2] Following standard practice (Kokko et al. 1996; Buckley et al. 2002; Liu 2008), one can also derive Eq (2.ii) using standard production function.

presence of FDI in the industrial sector of the state. We expect states with higher presence of FDI in the industrial sector to have higher levels of labour productivity, given other variables. Studies also link labour productivity with agglomeration effects and expect states with higher urbanisation and higher share of industries to enjoy higher productivity levels (Fujita et al. 1999; Rosenthal and Strange 2003; Audretsch and Lehmann 2005; Okada and Siddharthan 2008). Variables 4 and 5 have been introduced to capture this effect. Furthermore, some studies link labour productivity with exports. They argue that higher exports reveal international competitiveness and the use of state of the art technology. Variable 6 is used to capture this effect.

The following equations have been estimated:

$$\begin{aligned} LPL = {} & \alpha_0 + \alpha_1 FCL + \alpha_2 EDU14-18 + \alpha_3 FDI-FC + \alpha_4 IMR \\ & + \alpha_5 ISHARE + \alpha_6 X-INT + \alpha_7 URBTOT + u_1 \end{aligned} \tag{2.1}$$

$$\begin{aligned} LPE = {} & \beta_0 + \beta_1 FCE + \beta_2 EDU14-18 + \beta_3 FDI-FC + \beta_4 IMR \\ & + \beta_5 ISHARE + \beta_6 X-INT + \beta_7 URBTOT + u_2 \end{aligned} \tag{2.2}$$

$$\begin{aligned} GLPL = {} & \gamma_0 + \gamma_1 GFCL + \gamma_2 EDU14-18 + \gamma_3 FDI-FC + \gamma_4 IMR \\ & + \gamma_5 ISHARE + \gamma_6 X-INT + \gamma_7 URBTOT + u_3 \end{aligned} \tag{2.3}$$

$$\begin{aligned} GLPE = {} & \delta_0 + \delta_1 GFCE + \delta_2 EDU14-18 + \delta_3 FDI-FC + \delta_4 IMR \\ & + \delta_5 ISHARE + \delta_6 X-INT + \delta_7 URBTOT + u_4 \end{aligned} \tag{2.4}$$

$$\begin{aligned} GEMP = {} & \varepsilon_0 + \varepsilon_1 GFCL + \varepsilon_2 EDU14-18 + \varepsilon_3 GFDI + \varepsilon_4 ISHARE \\ & + \varepsilon_5 URBTOT + u_5 \end{aligned} \tag{2.5}$$

where all the five equations are based on the standard panel data regression model (Baltagi 2005).[3] The dependent variables in these five equations are labour productivity levels (LPL and LPE), growth in labour productivity (GLPL and GLPE) and growth in employment (GEMP). The explanatory variables are fixed capital-labour ratio (FCL and FCE), growth in fixed capital-labour ratio (GFCL and GFCE), skill content of the workforce in the state represented by the proxy variable of enrolment of children in schools in the age group of 14-18 (EDU14-18), foreign direct investments to fixed capital ratio (FDI-FC), infant mortality rate (IMR) representing the general quality of workforce in the state, agglomeration effects captured by industry share in the state's GDP (ISHARE), ratio of urban to total population (URBTOT) and international orientation of the state, namely, exports to state product ratio (export intensity X-INT). The definitions and the sources of data for these variables are discussed in the following section.

[3] For simplicity, the subscripts representing cross section and time for each of the variables have been dropped. We have used EViews7 software for estimation. We have assumed the presence of cross-sectional heteroscedasticity, and, hence, the econometric models have been estimated using feasible generalised least squares (FGLS) procedure allowing for cross-sectional fixed effects with cross-sectional weights.

We expect α_1, β_1, γ_1 and δ_1 to have positive signs indicating an increase in labour productivity consequent to an increase in capital stock. However, the sign of ε_1 could be negative as increase in capital stock need not result in an increase in employment. Growth of capital stock could result in a substitution of capital for labour, and this could result in a decline in the growth of employment.

We expect the coefficients of IMR in all the equations to be negative. Here, high infant mortality rate would indicate lower levels of health care and nutrition in the state. We expect higher labour productivity in states having a healthy labour force. The rest of the coefficients should have a positive sign as we expect education (influencing skill intensity of the labour force), FDI, exports, and agglomeration benefits indicated by urbanisation and share of industry in the state income to favourably influence labour productivity and employment.

2.4 Sample, Data and Variables

The sample used in this chapter is a balanced panel consisting of 21 states from India for a period of 5 years (2003–2007). These 21 states are Andhra Pradesh, Assam, Bihar, Chhattisgarh, Goa, Gujarat, Haryana, Himachal Pradesh, Jammu and Kashmir, Jharkhand, Karnataka, Kerala, Madhya Pradesh, Maharashtra, Orissa, Punjab, Rajasthan, Tamil Nadu, Uttarakhand, Uttar Pradesh and West Bengal. The union territories have been excluded as they have few manufacturing industries. Similarly, all the north-eastern states except Assam have been excluded for the same reason. The data sources used in the study are:

1. Value added, total persons engaged, total emoluments, fixed capital and net fixed capital formation (Source: The annual survey of industries (ASI))
2. Gross state domestic product (GSDP) at factor cost by industry of origin at current prices and share of industry in GSDP (Source: The national accounts data from central statistics office (CSO) under the Ministry of Statistics and Programme Implementation, Government of India)
3. State-wise gross enrolment ratios, state-wise stock of foreign direct investments, state-wise value of total exports and index numbers of wholesale prices (for all commodities and for machinery and machine tools) (Source: Indiastat.com)
4. Infant mortality rate (IMR) (Source: Various issues of sample registration system (SRS) bulletins from Registrar General)
5. State-wise distribution of urban and total population (Source: 'Population projections for India and states 2001–2026', report of the technical group on population projections constituted by the national commission on population May 2006, Office of the Registrar General & Census Commissioner, India)

The information collected through the above five sources have been used to construct the following variables for each of the 21 states:

LPL = labour productivity (definition 1) = net value added/total persons engaged
LPE = labour productivity (definition 2) = net value added/total emoluments

GLPL = growth in labour productivity (definition 1) = (labour productivity (definition 1) in current year – labour productivity (definition 1) in previous year)/labour productivity (definition 1) in previous year
GLPE = growth in labour productivity (definition 2) = (labour productivity (definition 2) in current year – labour productivity (definition 2) in previous year)/labour productivity (definition 2) in previous year
GEMP = growth in employment = (total persons engaged in current year – total persons engaged in previous year)/total persons engaged in previous year
FCL = fixed capital per labour = fixed capital/total persons engaged
FCE = fixed capital per unit cost of labour = fixed capital/total emoluments
GFCL = growth in fixed capital per labour = (fixed capital per labour in current year – fixed capital per labour in previous year)/fixed capital per labour in previous year
GFCE = growth in fixed capital per unit cost of labour = (fixed capital per unit cost of labour in current year – fixed capital per unit cost of labour in previous year)/fixed capital per unit cost of labour in previous year
EDU14-18 = skill = gross enrolment ratio in classes IX–XII (14–18 years)
FDI-FC = ratio of foreign direct investments to fixed capital = stock of foreign direct investments/fixed capital
GFDI = growth in foreign direct investments = (stock of foreign direct investments in current year – stock of foreign direct investments in previous year)/stock of foreign direct investments in previous year
IMR = infant mortality rate which is an indicator of the level of health = number of deaths of infants under 1 year old per 1,000 live births in a given year
ISHARE = industrialisation = amount of gross state domestic product due to industry sector/gross state domestic product
X-INT = international orientation of the state = value of total exports/gross state domestic product[4]
URBTOT = urbanisation = urban population/total population

The variables have been used in current and constant prices. Tables 2.1a and 2.2a present the results at current prices and Tables 2.1b and 2.2b at constant prices. In an era of fast technological changes, deflation by price index (constant prices) could create problems as index number of prices does not take into account changes in quality of the goods. The rapid increase in the use of numerically controlled machines and computer-aided manufacturing goes against the assumption of 'no change in quality' over the years. Hence, measuring variables at current prices would be more appropriate in the current era of rapid technological change. Nevertheless, we have also estimated the models using constant prices.[5] However, the results do not differ much in both the versions.

---

[4] Value of exports was available in the data source only for the years 2003, 2006 and 2007. Hence, first, the ratio of exports to gross state domestic product was calculated, and then the ratio was interpolated for the years 2004 and 2005 by considering a linear trend between 2003 and 2006.

[5] Labour productivity (definition 1) at constant prices has been calculated by deflating the net value added by the wholesale price index after shifting the index base to the year 2002–2003. Fixed capital has been calculated at constant prices using the perpetual inventory method (Liu 2008).

Table 2.1 Determinants of interstate differences in labour productivity

(a) At current prices

Panel EGLS (cross-sectional weights)

Equation	2.1	2.2	2.3	2.4
Variables	LPL	LPL	LPE	LPE
C	0.826	−19.651***	1.401	−13.379***
FCL	0.371***	0.259***		
FCE			0.193***	0.162**
EDU14-18	0.015*	0.024**	0.023*	0.044***
FDI-FC	0.922	−1.375	0.321	−1.418
IMR	−0.053***		−0.055**	
ISHARE	5.429**	3.799	8.401***	5.648**
X-INT	2.961***		2.630**	
URBTOT		0.697***		0.460***
R^2	0.929	0.945	0.884	0.898
NOBS	105	105	105	105

Note: *, **, *** significance at 10, 5 and 1% levels. LPL is labour productivity using number of workers, and LPE is labour productivity using emoluments (productivity per rupee spent on labour – inverse of efficiency wage)

(b) At constant prices with base year 2002–2003

Panel EGLS (cross-sectional weights)

Equation	2.1	2.2
Variables	LPL	LPL
C	0.667	−10.048***
FCL	0.208***	0.214***
EDU14-18	0.014	0.021**
FDI-FC	−0.997	−1.681 **
IMR	−0.021	
ISHARE	5.493***	2.861*
X-INT	2.09***	
URBTOT		0.373***
R^2	0.936	0.955
NOBS	105	105

Note: *, **, *** significance at 10, 5 and 1 % levels. LPL is labour productivity using number of workers

2.5 Results

The panel model results of generalised least squares using cross-sectional weights are presented in Tables 2.1 and 2.2. Table 2.1a and b present the results of determinants of interstate differences of labour productivity. Similarly, Table 2.2a and b present the results of determinants of growth of labour productivity and growth of employment.

As discussed in the earlier sections, two definitions of labour productivity have been used in the study: 1. value added per number of workers and 2. value added by

Table 2.2 Determinants of interstate differences in the growth of labour productivity and employment

(a) At current prices

Panel EGLS (cross-sectional weights)

Equation	2.1	2.2	2.3
	GLPL	GLPE	GEMP
C	5.100***	4.044***	–2.980***
GFCL	0.399**		–0.145***
GFCE		0.606***	
EDU14-18	0.014***	0.014***	0.0017**
FDI-FC/GFDI†	0.968*	1.088**	–0.002***
IMR	–0.034***	–0.029***	
ISHARE			0.245**
X-INT	0.374	0.364	
URBTOT	–0.147***	–0.120***	0.104***
R^2	0.706	0.766	0.803
NOBS	84	84	84

Note: *, **,*** significance at 10, 5 and 1% levels. GFDI† is relevant to GEMP equations. GLPL is growth of labour productivity using number of workers. GLPE is growth of labour productivity using emoluments (productivity per rupee spent on labour – inverse of efficiency wage)

(b) At constant prices with base year 2002–2003)

Panel EGLS (cross-sectional weights)

Equation	2.1	2.2
	GLPL	GEMP
C	3.230***	–2.967***
GFCL	0.237	–0.359***
EDU14-18	0.012***	0.003***
FDI-FC/GFDI†	0.789	–0.003***
IMR	–0.023**	
ISHARE		0.486***
X-INT	0.395	
URBTOT	–0.097***	0.099***
R^2	0.646	0.873
NOBS	84	84

Note: *, **, *** significance at 10, 5 and 1% levels. GFDI† is relevant to GEMP equations. GLPL is growth of labour productivity using number of workers

wages and salaries paid to employees, that is, productivity of rupee spent on workers. In Table 2.1a, Eqs. 2.1 and 2.2 present the determinants of LPL (value added per labour) and Eqs. 2.3 and 2.4 present determinants of LPE (productivity of rupee spent on labour). All the statistically significant coefficients in Table 2.1a have expected signs. As anticipated, capital intensity as measured by FCL or FCE is an important determinant of labour productivity and has a positive sign. States that have a higher share of urban population and industrialisation enjoy higher productivities due to agglomeration advantages. Furthermore, the states where the firms export more also experience higher productivities. The crucial role of human capital in influencing labour productivity is revealed in Table 2.1a and b. After controlling for other determinants, variables representing human capital status in the state, namely, percentage of population in the age group of 14–18 attending schools and the health and nutrition indicator represented by infant mortality rate, emerge significant determinants of productivity.

Most of these results hold true even when the regression models are estimated with labour productivity and fixed capital-labour ratio at constant prices. The only striking difference that emerges is with regard to the statistically significant negative coefficient on FDI-FC variable in Eq. 2.2 of Table 2.1b. Having established this, we wish to investigate whether human capital also influences growth of productivity and employment among states. Table 2.2 deals with these issues.

In Table 2.2a, the first two equations deal with the growth of labour productivity and the third equation with the growth of employment. The results of the GLPL and GLPE equations are similar. The growth of fixed capital strongly influences labour productivity and the influence is stronger in the GLPE equation. Urbanisation variable has a negative sign, perhaps indicating catching-up of the productivity levels by units in less urban states.

Human capital variable, namely, high school enrolment rate, is significant in the growth of productivity equations also. Thus, higher enrolments in high schools contribute not only to higher labour productivity but also to higher growth in productivity. This result brings out the crucial role played by the human capital variable in enhancing productivity and its growth. Furthermore, IMR has a strong negative influence on the growth of productivity. Thus, states that have been spending on health and hygiene and having healthier population have been experiencing higher productivity growth rates. The policy implication is that the states need to invest in human capital to enhance productivity levels, and without enhancing productivity levels, per capita income cannot be enhanced and sustained. Thus, mere investment in physical capital is not sufficient and investment in human capital is a must.

Equation 2.3 of Table 2.2a deals with the growth of employment. Increase in capital intensity (GFCL) affects employment adversely due to the substitution of capital for labour. Growth of employment is more in the urbanised states and in the industrialised states. However, FDI does not seem to contribute to the growth of employment. What is more important and of immediate concern for our chapter is that education variable has a positive impact on employment growth. Thus, states that have higher high school enrolment rates have been enjoying higher growth rates of employment.

On the whole, the results presented show strong skill bias in productivity and employment growths. Consequently, states that have been neglecting universal high school education are likely to become victims in the sense they will experience less growth of employment and productivity. They go down on both counts.

2.6 Conclusions

This study shows that after controlling for fixed capital, human capital, in the form of higher education and health infrastructure, is emerging as a significant contributor for labour productivity, its growth and growth of employment.

Labour productivity is high in states where a large proportion of children go to high and higher secondary schools. Likewise, states with healthier population have higher labour productivity. In addition, agglomeration effects are also very important. In particular, urbanisation and industrial agglomeration have external economies influencing labour productivity levels.

The results on growth of productivity reinforce the conclusions drawn on the levels of productivity. In addition to the growth of capital stock, states that enjoy higher proportion of higher secondary school enrolment and healthier populations experience higher productivity growth.

The growth of employment has also been high in states where human capital is more developed. In other words, in states where few children go to high and higher secondary schools, the employment growth is low. Employment is also favourably affected by urbanisation and agglomeration effects. The results of this chapter show that while growth of capital stock positively influences productivity growth, the same is not expected to favour employment growth.

The study by and large supports the skill bias in the current technological revolution where both employment and productivity grow faster in states that are endowed with better human capital. States that have been ignoring secondary and higher secondary education and health care seem to have become victims of the current technological revolution. Mere concentration on enhancing physical capital will not lead to a sustainable growth in employment and income.

Acknowledgement We are grateful to Saumitra Bhaduri, K. S. Kavi Kumar, K. R. Shanmugam and Brinda Viswanathan for several helpful comments and suggestions.

References

Audretsch DB, Lehmann EE (2005) Does the knowledge spillover theory of entrepreneurship hold for regions? Res Policy 34(8):1191–1202

Baltagi BH (2005) Econometric analysis of panel data, 3rd edn. Wiley, Chichester

Buckley PJ, Clegg J, Wang C (2002) The impact of inward FDI on the performance of Chinese manufacturing firms. J Int Bus Stud 33(4):637–655

Caves RE (1992) Industrial efficiency in six nations. MIT Press, Cambridge, MA

Ciccone A, Papaioannou E (2009) Human capital, the structure of production, and growth. Rev Econ Stat 91(1):66–82

Doctor M (2007) Boosting investment and growth: the role of social pacts in the Brazilian automotive industry. Oxf Dev Stud 35(1):105–30

Epifani P, Gancia G (2008) The skill bias of world trade. Econ J 118(530):927–60

Feliciano ZM (2001) Workers and trade liberalization: the impact of trade reforms in Mexico on wages and employment. Ind Labor Relat Rev 55(1):95–115

Fujita M, Krugman P, Venables AJ (1999) The spatial economy: cities, regions, and international trade. MIT Press, Cambridge, MA

Gao T (2005) Labor quality and the location of foreign direct investment: evidence from China. China Econ Rev 16(3):274–92

Grossman GM, Helpman E (1991) Innovation and growth in the global economy. MIT Press, Cambridge, MA

Harrison R (2008) Skill-based technology adoption: firm-level evidence from Brazil and India. Institute for Fiscal Studies, IFS working papers: W08/03

Helpman E (ed) (1998) General purpose technologies and economic growth. MIT Press, Cambridge, MA

Jung JH, Choi K (2006) The labor market structure of knowledge-based industries: a Korean case. J Asia Pac Econ 11(1):59–78

Kathuria V (2002) Liberalisation, FDI and productivity spillovers – an analysis of Indian manufacturing firms. Oxf Econ Pap 54:688–718

Kim KS (1998) Global integration, capital and labor: a north–south comparative perspective. In: Dabir-Alai P, Odekon M (eds) Economic liberalization and labor markets. Greenwood Press, Westport, pp 25–44

Kokko A, Tansini R, Zejan MC (1996) Local technological capability and productivity spillovers from FDI in the Uruguayan manufacturing sector. J Dev Stud 32(4):602–611

Liu Z (2008) Foreign direct investment and technology spillovers: theory and evidence. J Dev Econ 85(1–2):176–193

Maiti D, Mitra A (2010) Skills, informality, and development. IEG working paper no. 306

Mankiw NG, Romer D, Weil DN (1992) A contribution to empirics of economic growth. Q J Econ 107(2):407–37

Noorbakhsh F, Paloni A, Youssef A (2001) Human capital and FDI inflows to developing countries: new empirical evidence. World Dev 29(9):1593–1610

Okada A, Siddharthan NS (2008) Automobile clusters in India: evidence from Chennai and the national capital region. In: Kuchiki A, Tsuji M (eds) The flowchart approach to industrial cluster policy. Palgrave-Macmillan, London, pp 109–144

Pandit BL, Siddharthan NS (2008) MNEs, product differentiation, skills and employment: lessons from the Indian experience. In: Hashim SR, Siddharthan NS (eds) High tech industries, employment and global competitiveness. Routledge, New Delhi, pp 165–179

Ray S (2004) MNEs, strategic alliances and efficiency of firms: emerging trends. Econ Polit Wkly 39(5):434–40

Romer PM (1994) The origins of endogenous growth. J Econ Perspect 8(1):3–22

Rosenthal SS, Strange WC (2003) Geography, industrial organization and agglomeration. Rev Econ Stat 85(2):377–393

Salvanes KG, Forre ES (2003) Effects on employment of trade and technical change: evidence from Norway. Economica 70:293–329

Siddharthan NS, Lal K (2004) Liberalisation, MNE and productivity of Indian enterprises. Econ Polit Wkly 39(5):448–452

Yeaple SR (2003) The role of skill endowments in the structure of U.S. outward foreign direct investment. Rev Econ Stat 85(3):726–34

Yussof I, Ismail R (2002) Human resource competitiveness and inflow of foreign direct investment to the ASEAN region. Asia-Paci Develop J 9(1):89–107

Chapter 3
Impact of Human Capital on Manufacturing Productivity Growth in India

Vinish Kathuria, S.N. Rajesh Raj, and Kunal Sen

3.1 Introduction

It is well established that long-term growth and development across countries is driven to a large extent by productivity growth (Easterly and Levine 2001). Several studies exist that have attempted to examine the effect of different factors influencing productivity growth using industries or firms as units of analysis. Most of these studies highlight the role of trade openness, research and development (R&D) and market structure as major determinants of industry or firm productivity growth (see, e.g. Bartelsman and Doms 2000; Harriss 1999; Tybout 2000; Chand and Sen 2002; Goldar and Kumari 2003; Isaksson 2007; Mitra and Ural 2007). A considerable body of research has also concentrated on the role of human capital investment in explaining the level and variation in production and earnings in the manufacturing sector (Batra and Tan 2000; Dearden et al. 2000; Jones 2001; Takii 2003; Ilmakunnas et al. 2004; Nielsen and Rosholm 2002). While there has been significant amount of literature examining the contribution of human capital to firm growth and productivity, we are not aware of any study that has attempted to analyse the contribution of human capital (proxied by education) on productivity growth of the manufacturing firms in India, especially at the subnational (state) level. Taking cognizance of it, this chapter examines the role of human capital formation proxied by literacy in explaining productivity growth across industries.

V. Kathuria (✉)
SJMSOM, Indian Institute of Technology Bombay, Mumbai, India
e-mail: vinish@iitb.ac.in

S.N. Rajesh Raj
Centre for Multi-Disciplinary Development Research, Dharwad, India
e-mail: rajeshraj.natarajan@gmail.com

K. Sen
IDPM, University of Manchester, Manchester, UK
e-mail: Kunal.Sen@manchester.ac.uk

N.S. Siddharthan and K. Narayanan (eds.), *Human Capital and Development: The Indian Experience*, DOI 10.1007/978-81-322-0857-0_3, © Springer India 2013

It is argued that education plays a significant role in a rapidly changing work environment due to technological advances (Welch 1970; Mincer 1989; Hellerstein and Neumark 2004). The ability of workers to process new information becomes increasingly important in an environment of technological advancement. According to this view, the better educated workers enjoy comparative advantage in adapting to new technologies than less educated ones. As a result, productivity of better educated workers is relatively greater than the less educated ones (Bartel and Lichtenberg 1987; Tan and Lopez-Acevedo 2002; Hellerstein and Neumark 2004). In this chapter, we use the human capital framework to examine the relationship between education and total factor productivity growth (TFPG) in the manufacturing sector in India by using industries as units of analysis. Our empirical context is Indian manufacturing, and we examine whether the variation in TFPG for the same set of industries across Indian states and over time can be related to variations in literacy levels across these states.

We first measure TFPG using Levinsohn and Petrin (LP) method for the 15 major Indian states for the period 1994–2005. We then exploit the differences in human capital formation across Indian states (as measured by literacy level) to examine the effects of education on total factor productivity growth.

Our chapter has two important methodological strengths. First, we are able to test for the impact of human capital on TFPG for the combined manufacturing sector, which includes both the formal and informal segments of the manufacturing sector. Previous studies on TFPG in Indian manufacturing have estimated TFPG only for the formal manufacturing sector. This is a serious omission as nearly 35% of output and 85% of employment in Indian manufacturing are in the informal sector (Mukherjee 2004). A second strength of the empirical analysis is that we use the Levinsohn-Petrin method of calculating TFPG, which addresses the simultaneity bias in standard productivity estimates.

The remaining chapter is organised in five sections. Section 3.2 summarises the theoretical and empirical literature on determinants of productivity growth and discusses the importance of the role of human capital in enhancing productivity. Section 3.3 describes the methodologies, both in estimating TFPG and in testing for the effect of human capital on TFPG. This is followed by a description of the data and variables used in the empirical analysis in Sect. 3.4. The section then provides the estimates of TFPG calculations. Section 3.5 provides the results of the TFP growth estimations, where we test for the effects of human capital formation on TFPG. Section 3.6 concludes.

3.2 What Determines Productivity Growth in Industry?[1]

The literature has proposed various potential determinants of firm productivity. These include trade and openness, ownership, role of institutions such as labour market, fairness in dealings, public investment in health, human capital, physical infrastructure leading to better quality of workforce, research and development (R&D), business environment, etc.

[1] This section builds on Kathuria et al. (2011).

Table 3.1 Productivity (in Rs.) variation across the states for the same industries for 3 years

Industry	Year = 1994	Year = 2000	Year = 2005
Pump, compressors and valves	0.76–33,256	0.32–46,948	0.15–38,212
Agriculture and forestry machinery	0.61–170,326.1	0.39–433,879	0.09–324,703
Machine tools	0.46–50,028	0.94–23,424	0.66–42,884
Food-, beverage- and tobacco-processing machinery	1.41–43,145	0.72–40,504	0.63–30,971
Domestic appliances	0.50–31,502	1.23–24,931	0.31–38,935

Source: Kathuria et al. (2009)

Studies suggest positive effect of trade and openness on industrial productivity (see, e.g. Devarajan and Rodrik 1991; Rodrik 1992; Melitz 2003; Krugman and Obstfeld 2005; Mitra and Ural 2007; Kathuria 2008, among others). Several studies highlight a beneficial effect of exports on firm TFP (Kraay 1999; Blalock and Gertler 2004; Fernandes and Isgut 2006). Empirical evidence also exists for the positive impact of R&D activities on firm productivity (Griliches 1998; Kathuria 2008). Recent literature has also focused on the role of the business environment for firm TFP (Hallward-Driemeier et al. 2003; Dollar et al. 2005; Wagner 2007) and the effects of foreign ownership on firm TFP (Arnold and Javorcik 2005; Kee 2005). According to Mitra and Ural (2007) and Iskasson (2007), quality of public infrastructure is also a significant factor influencing factor productivity. Another policy variable that has effect on the efficiency of the firms is the prevailing competitive condition in the sector. A restriction on free entry and exit of firms hinders competition faced by existing firms and thus lowers firm efficiency (Mitra and Ural 2007).

Schultz (1961) and Becker (1964) have drawn attention to the significant role human capital plays in improving earnings and growth. There is overwhelming evidence at the micro level, particularly at the firm and worker level, that education and training proxied by experience enhance productivity and hence earnings. Studies by Batra and Tan (2000), Dearden et al. (2000), Jones (2001), Takii (2003), Tan and Lopez-Acevedo (2002), Aw et al. (2005) and Ilmakunnas et al. (2004) found positive influence of human capital on firm's TFP. A number of studies have also examined the impact of education on worker's earnings (Jones 2001; Takii 2003) and found a positive relationship between them.

It can be clearly seen that some of the determinants discussed are determined nationally – e.g. trade, R&D and competition policies – and hence need to be controlled for, either explicitly (trade/competition) or indirectly via fixed effects (R&D). Still, nationally governed variables or industry fixed effects cannot explain why productivity and productivity growth for the same industry differ across regions. Any productivity difference or productivity growth difference for the same industry across the region/states thus would be due to the presence of varied human capital base across states. This is well illustrated in Table 3.1, which gives the range of productivity for some of the key industries across Indian states.

The table indicates wide variation in productivity across the industries. Apparently no study exists in the Indian context that has looked into the role of human capital in affecting productivity. The present study fills this obvious gap.

3.3 Methodology

3.3.1 Growth Equation Estimation

In this chapter, an attempt is made to statistically establish the relationship between human capital and TFPG. The following regression function is estimated separately for combined, formal and informal sectors.

$$\mathrm{TFPG}_{ist}^{I,F,C} = a_0 + a_1 X_{it} + L_{st} + T + e_{ist} \tag{3.1}$$

The subscripts i, s and t index the industry, state and time period. TFPG is total factor productivity growth, X is a vector that includes other determinants of TFPG such as trade and competition variables, L is the period-averaged measure of literacy level for state s at time t (where t=1994–2001 and 2001–2006) and T is the time dummy, which is equal to 1 when t=2001–2006 and 0, otherwise. e_{ist} is the state-industry-time error term. I, F and C represent informal, formal and combined sectors, respectively.

The trade and competition policy variables used as controls for the above growth equation estimation are the import penetration and export orientation ratios, tariff rates and the Herfindahl-Hirschman Index (HHI) at the four digit level. We however could not directly control for the R&D intensity but used industry dummies in one of the specifications to see the effect of any industry-specific policies. The inclusion of a year dummy, T, is to capture macroeconomic shocks to capacity utilisation, which may affect TFP over time.

We test the relationship separately for formal and informal manufacturing sector due to the existence of duality in the Indian manufacturing sector. The Indian manufacturing sector consists of two categories of firms depending on the size of the labour force in the firm – formal and informal sectors. Firms which are in the formal sector are required to adhere to various regulatory norms besides providing several benefits to the workers.[2] Apart from this, the reservation of few products for small-scale units and tax benefits to them has resulted in duality in Indian manufacturing (Mazumdar and Sarkar 2008). Second, available evidence suggests that the unorganised manufacturing sector suffers from low levels of productivity and efficiency owing to the presence of large pool of low-skilled and less educated workers, inferior technology and low wages. Research studies have recommended that measures such as technological upgradation and strengthening the link between organised and unorganised sectors could help in improving the efficiency of the sector (Mukherjee 2004; Raj and Duraisamy 2005; Raj 2006). As technological upgradation could be

[2] The formal (referred as organised) sector in India is defined to be the set of firms who are required to be registered under the Factories Act (1948). By doing so, they fall under the purview of labour laws and other government regulations. The registration in Factories Act is mandatory if they employ 10 workers and use electricity or 20 workers but do not use electricity. The remaining firms, which do not require registration, are called as the informal (referred as unorganised) sector firms.

a costly measure especially for firms in the informal sector, improving skills of the workforce to handle the existing, if not better, technology could bring in desired changes in productivity and efficiency of the sector (Majumdar 2004). Thus, testing the relationship for formal and informal manufacturing in a way would be a test for this duality and validity of the scope and importance of human capital formation for these two segments of the manufacturing sector.

3.3.2 TFPG Estimation

3.3.2.1 Levinsohn and Petrin (LP) Methodology[3]

For finding TFPG, we estimate the Cobb-Douglas (CD) production function in Equation (3.2) separately for each of the 15 major Indian states. The states included are Andhra Pradesh (AP), Assam, Bihar, Gujarat, Haryana, Karnataka, Kerala, Madhya Pradesh (MP), Maharashtra, Orissa, Punjab, Rajasthan, Tamil Nadu (TN), Uttar Pradesh (UP) and West Bengal (WB).

$$\ln Y_{ijt} = A_{it} + \beta_L \ln L_{ijt} + \beta_K \ln K_{ijt} \tag{3.2}$$

The subscript i indexes the state, j indexes the industry and t indexes the time period. The variables Y, L and K represent the real value added, labour and capital input, respectively. A is TFP which represents the efficiency of the firm in transforming inputs into output.

The estimation of Eq. (3.2) using ordinary least squares (OLS) method does not correct for the endogeneity bias generally associated with the production function estimations. We corrected for the potential simultaneity bias generated by firm time-varying unobservables by employing a methodology developed by Levinsohn and Petrin (2003). The main idea behind this methodology is that an observable firm characteristic can be used to proxy for the unobserved firm productivity and estimate unbiased production function coefficients. We used intermediate inputs as the proxy to address this bias (Kathuria et al. 2010).

3.4 Data and Variables

3.4.1 Data for the Productivity Estimation

This study uses firm-level data for both formal and informal manufacturing sectors. The data for the informal manufacturing sector are drawn from the National Sample Survey Organisation (NSSO) surveys on the informal manufacturing sector for

[3] Refer to Kathuria et al. (2009, 2010) for detailed discussion on the methodology.

1994–1995, 2000–2001 and 2005–2006. Data for the same 3 years for the formal sector are obtained from the Annual Survey of Industries (ASI). It is important to note here that at the time of the analysis, the unit-level ASI data for 2005–2006 was yet to be released. On account of it, we have considered the ASI dataset for the year 2004–2005. We have aggregated the unit-level data to arrive at the four-digit industry-level data for each state. To implement the Levinsohn-Petrin methodology, we constructed a panel of four-digit industries for the period 1994–1995 to 2005–2006. While constructing the panel, we omitted units that reported zero or negative capital stock, zero output and zero employment.[4]

3.4.2 Variables

The variables used in TFP estimates are output, labour, capital and intermediate inputs. To make the values of output, capital and intermediate inputs comparable over time and across industries and states, suitable deflators have been used. Gross value added (GVA) is used as the measure of output, which is constructed using single deflation method. We used the industry-specific wholesale price index as the output price deflator. The capital input is represented by gross fixed assets. To arrive at real fixed assets, we used wholesale price index (WPI) for machinery and machine tools as the deflator. Total number of persons engaged is our labour input.

3.4.3 Data for the Growth Equation Estimation

In this chapter, we examine the relationship between human capital and manufacturing productivity. The human capital in our study is represented by adult literacy level. We argue that improvement in literacy over time in a state would enhance the overall human capital base in the sector, thereby creating a positive impact on productivity growth. Data on adult literacy rate were obtained from various issues of educational statistics published by the Ministry of Human Resources and Development (MHRD), New Delhi.

Import penetration and export orientation ratios, tariff rates and the Herfindahl-Hirschman index (HHI) are used as control variables in the TFP growth equation estimation. Data on export orientation, import penetration and tariff rates (both simple and weighted tariff) came from Nicita and Olarreaga (2006). These data are at the three-digit ISIC level and are matched to the NIC two-digit industry level. Exports and imports data are converted to Indian rupees using the dollar-rupee

[4] In 2000, Bihar, MP and UP were bifurcated and three new states – Uttarakhand, Chhattisgarh and Jharkhand – were formed; for the present analysis, these three states were merged with their parent states so as to have consistent data for all the three time periods.

Table 3.2 Average values for human capital, trade and competition variables

	Variable	1994–2000	2001–2005
1.	Literacy	60.89	67.85
		(10.88)	(9.19)
2.	Change in literacy	7.60	6.34
		(2.91)	(2.43)
3.	SIMTF	41.82	39.12
		(21.805)	(18.537)
4.	WHTTF	46.13	43.20
		(36.094)	(31.907)
5.	HHI	0.17	0.164
		(0.108)	(0.103)
6.	IMPEN	0.096	0.096
		(0.138)	(0.138)
7.	EXPOR	0.132	0.0398
		(0.189)	(0.064)

Note: Figures in parentheses are standard deviation

exchange rates obtained from the RBI. These figures are then deflated using WPI for manufactured products at the two-digit industry level. Data on HHI are drawn from the PROWESS database of the Centre for Monitoring Indian Economy (CMIE).

Table 3.2 presents the summary statistics. We can infer the following: (a) there is a considerable improvement in literacy rate over time (row 1); (b) trade restrictions on the manufacturing sector has lessened over time, as evident by the decrease in tariffs (rows 3–4), though this has not led to increased import penetration or export orientation (rows 6 and 7); and (c) competition has increased in the Indian manufacturing sector, as evident from the decline in HHI (row 5).

3.4.4 Productivity Growth Estimates

This section discusses the productivity trends at the subnational level. Tables 3.3, 3.4, and 3.5 give the TFPG[5] estimates for formal, informal and combined manufacturing sectors, respectively. A steady growth in TFP is observed for the formal manufacturing sector in the period 1994–2005 (Table 3.3). A comparison of TFPG during 1994–2001 and 2001–2005 suggests a surge in TFP growth in the latter period as compared to the former. TFPG grew at a rate of 0.04% per annum in the first period and 3.1% in the second period. We also find that the aggregate growth conceals considerable variation in productivity growth at the regional level.

[5] It is to be noted that wherever growth rate has been computed in Table 3.3 or elsewhere, it is the compound annual growth rate (CAGR) for the period. The CAGR is calculated as $[(Y_t/Y_0)^{(1/t)}-1]*100$, where Y_t and Y_0 are the terminal and initial values of the variable and t is the time over which CAGR has to be calculated.

Table 3.3 Total factor productivity growth in the formal sector

	1994–2001		2001–2005		1994–2005	
State	Mean	SD	Mean	SD	Mean	SD
Punjab	1.74	22.81	2.22	21.7	3.04	10.64
Haryana	−2.97	22.43	2.56	31.47	−1.79	15.7
Rajasthan	−0.73	22.46	1.09	36.87	−1.96	22.38
UP	−1.28	19.05	6.65	24.24	1.29	10.53
Bihar	−0.94	24.71	−3.8	27.02	−5.24	22.16
Assam	3.89	32.78	1.66	22.33	4.06	10.34
WB	−0.59	14.37	4.82	42.77	−0.94	14.16
Orissa	−0.08	16.07	1.23	27.11	−0.69	18.37
MP	6.31	28.54	0.71	22.14	4.69	11.58
Gujarat	5.52	30.34	0.74	29.15	5.2	17.9
Maharashtra	−6.17	8.86	5.14	17.08	−1.64	6.63
AP	−1.32	11.87	9.57	40.13	1.71	7.5
Karnataka	−0.16	20.34	8.2	51.56	2.83	10.95
Kerala	0.47	14.12	3.13	20.09	−0.31	12.1
TN	−3.11	11.54	3.25	24.25	−0.58	6.91
Mean	*0.04*		*3.14*		*0.64*	

Notes: estimated from the data without outliers (On checking standard deviation of TFPG, it was found that for some states, few industries were influencing TFPG. The present table gives TFPG estimates after omitting these industries. For the TFPG estimates from the data with outliers, refer to Kathuria et al. (2010))

Table 3.4 Total factor productivity growth in the informal sector

	1994–2001		2001–2005		1994–2005	
State	Mean	SD	Mean	SD	Mean	SD
Punjab	−7.69	10.39	−3.72	24.57	−6.25	12.02
Haryana	−8.91	10.55	−11.04	21.26	−10.63	10.69
Rajasthan	−7.6	10.23	−11.48	20.51	−9.96	10.1
UP	−2.8	21.58	4.44	20.83	0.6	9.51
Bihar	0.74	24.26	−13.75	31.26	−8.48	22.2
Assam	−3.89	10.92	−32.52	12.27	−18.33	7.73
WB	−4.54	8.49	−10.75	21.38	−8.48	10.55
Orissa	−6.67	10.4	−34.18	9.74	−20.29	4.59
MP	7.99	32.95	−4.06	23.38	4.92	14.92
Gujarat	−2.51	12.06	−19.38	16.9	−10.7	8.83
Maharashtra	−2.45	10.22	−4.74	22.7	−4.03	12.06
AP	−3.08	9.88	−26.98	16.26	−14.73	9.08
Karnataka	−3.64	10.79	−26.52	15.2	−15.26	9.52
Kerala	−13.7	12.39	−22.21	14.3	−17.94	8.89
TN	−1.42	6.96	−23.14	19.21	−12.59	9.63
Mean	*−4.01*		*−16.0*		*−10.14*	

Notes: Same as Table 3.3

The TFP growth in the informal manufacturing sector presents a different story (Table 3.4). TFP has steadily declined in the sector over the period 1994–2005. The decline that began in 1994–2001 continued in the second period too. The sector

Table 3.5 Total factor productivity growth in the combined sector (formal + informal)

	1994–2001		2001–2005		1994–2005	
States	Mean	SD	Mean	SD	Mean	SD
Punjab	−0.46	21.06	−1.46	23.45	0.73	10.46
Haryana	−5.69	22.1	0.61	26.55	−3.34	14.82
Rajasthan	−0.8	22.95	−0.69	28.06	−1.29	17.82
Uttar Pradesh	−1.27	19.06	4.74	19.11	1.08	9.57
Bihar	−0.68	24.38	−6.04	22.21	−5.98	20.57
Assam	3.02	32.01	−8.31	24.58	−1.39	13.63
West Bengal	−1.96	13.13	1.4	27.84	−1.94	13.19
Orissa	0.9	26.45	−6.35	25.85	−4.54	18.83
Madhya Pradesh	2.8	26.49	2.27	18.62	3.52	9.86
Gujarat	−0.79	26.27	24.8	219.8	2.36	15.66
Maharashtra	−6.37	9.58	3.38	14.79	−1.39	6.73
Andhra Pradesh	−2.42	12.19	4.94	31.77	−0.12	8.39
Karnataka	−0.7	14.81	2.42	25.89	1.16	8.99
Kerala	−4.32	11.83	1.35	18.78	−3.31	12.03
Tamil Nadu	−3.63	11.34	0.74	21.73	−1.1	6.49
Mean	*−1.49*		*1.59*		*−1.04*	

Notes: Same as Table 3.3

witnessed a huge fall in TFP by 16% in the period 2001–2005. We observe less regional variation in TFPG in the informal sector with majority of the states registering TFP decline in both the periods.

When we bundled the formal and informal manufacturing sector together, a turnaround in TFP is noticed in the second period, 2001–2006 (Table 3.5). TFP switched over from a negative growth of 1.5% per annum in 1995–2001 to a positive growth rate of 1.6% per annum during 2001–2006.

3.5 Estimation of the TFPG Growth Equation: Results

We begin with the results for the combined manufacturing sector (Table 3.6). The results are presented for the relative change in explanatory variables (i.e. log differences) rather than the absolute values. Our choice of log differences over absolute values is due to the fact that any productivity shock in a period will be governed more by the changed trade regime or competition instead of the actual regime.[6] Our education variable is period-averaged measure of adult literacy rate.

Our results unambiguously state that education (Table 3.6, row 1) is a key factor explaining TFP growth of Indian industry (Model 1). None of the control variables (trade and competition variables) are significant (rows 2–4). The less important role

[6] We also used these variables in average form and the beginning of the period; the results are not reported but in all these models, the SBR variable hardly changed.

Table 3.6 Human capital and productivity growth across Indian states, robust estimations: combined manufacturing sector

	Variables	Model 1	Model 2	Model 3 (IV)
1.	Literacy	1.48*	0.27*	0.26*
		(0.39)	(0.14)	(0.14)
2.	HHI	–9.80	7.23	7.15
		(35.46)	(20.15)	(31.19)
3.	IMPEN	−185.75	18.16	18.49
		(158.43)	(86.32)	(42.41)
4.	EXPOR	40.89	2.50	2.67
		(56.88)	(38.32)	(41.80)
5.	Outlier	–	2981.83*	2981.92*
			(290.49)	(42.01)
6.	Year effect	Yes	Yes	Yes
7.	Industry effects	–	–	–
8.	R squared	0.02	0.75	0.75
9.	N	1,751	1,751	1,751

Notes: *indicates significance at minimum 10% level
Figures in the parentheses are standard errors; the results are obtained after correcting for heteroskedasticity if any

of trade variables in influencing productivity can be gauged from the fact that major trade reforms were carried out in 1991, and that tariff rates had fallen quite sharply by 1994.[7] Another reason could be the level of disaggregation of trade variables, which being at three-digit level, whereas TFPG is computed at the four-digit level. Same is the case with HHI, which too has been computed at the three-digit level.

It is possible that a few industries having very high TFPG might be driving the results on the impact of education on productivity growth. The inclusion of a dummy for these outlier industries (Model 2) improves our estimates and the explanatory power of the model.

3.5.1 *Testing for Potential Endogeneity*

One potential concern with our results is that the literacy variable may be endogenous to productivity growth. States with a literate and more educated workforce are likely to be more efficient because of their greater ability to absorb and effectively utilise new technology. Also, the presence of more literate workforce in a particular state (or particular region in a state such as Bangalore, Mumbai, Delhi, Chennai and so on) may lead to more productive firms from other states to relocate to that state.

[7] The maximum tariff for a large number of industries which was varying between 100 and 355% in 1990 fell to 65% in 1992 for almost all the industries except for beverages, iron and steel and industrial chemicals (Nicita and Olarreaga 2006).

Table 3.7 Human capital and productivity growth across Indian states, robust estimations: formal manufacturing sector

	Variables	Model 1	Model 2	Model 3 (IV)
1.	Literacy	3.45*	1.02*	0.97*
		(1.09)	(0.52)	(0.53)
2.	HHI	−30.16	62.30	60.86
		(73.10)	(83.25)	(119.20)
3.	IMPEN	−201.92	110.48	116.46
		(412.63)	(314.21)	(157.70)
4.	EXPOR	−0.35	26.19	29.43
		(121.59)	(139.93)	(158.81)
5.	Outlier	–	6113.18*	6114.85*
			(1057.93)	(155.06)
6.	Year effect	Yes	Yes	Yes
7.	Industry effects	–	–	–
8.	*R* squared	0.02	0.49	0.49
9.	*N*	1,687	1,687	1,687

Notes: *indicates significance at minimum 10% level

Two sets of instruments are used to control for the potential endogeneity of the literacy variable: one based on land reform legislation enacted by Indian states in different points in time and the other based on the nature of the political regime in a given state.[8]

Model 3 in Table 3.6 presents the results of the instrument variable (IV) estimation. The coefficients for literacy and other variables however do not change, indicating that endogeneity is not a problem with our estimations. This is also verified by Wooldridge's (1995) robust score test, which is not significant, thereby rejecting endogeneity.

3.5.2 Effect of Human Capital on Formal and Informal Manufacturing

The results thus indicate that literacy has a positive impact on the TFP growth of Indian industry. However, it is possible that the effect may vary between formal and informal sectors due to the differences in the characteristics of the workforce they employ. As argued earlier, the informal sector is alleged to be a reservoir of less-skilled and low-educated workforce, while the formal sector employs mostly skilled workforce. Thus, it is possible that the contribution of education will be significantly higher in the formal sector as compared to the informal sector. In other words, the effect of literacy should be mainly on the formal manufacturing; the informal sector is less likely to benefit from this variable. Thus, it is important to carry out estimations for formal and informal manufacturing sector separately. Tables 3.7 and 3.8 give

[8] For detailed discussion on these instruments, kindly refer to Kathuria et al. (2009).

Table 3.8 Human capital and productivity growth across Indian states, robust estimations: informal manufacturing sector

	Variables	Model 1	Model 2	Model 3 (IV)
1.	Literacy	0.17	–0.06	–0.07
		(0.18)	(0.06)	(0.12)
2.	HHI	–42.49*	9.97*	9.69*
		(22.16)	(5.66)	(24.18)
3.	IMPEN	36.32	22.00	23.87
		(102.00)	(39.69)	(36.30)
4.	EXPOR	96.44*	–13.27	–12.46
		(45.82)	(15.38)	(33.81)
5.	Outlier	–	3276.33*	3276.53*
			(610.49)	(54.53)
6.	Year effect	Yes	Yes	Yes
7.	Industry effects	–	–	–
8.	*R* squared	0.01	0.74	0.74
9.	*N*	1,291	1,291	1,291

Note: *indicates significance at minimum 10% level

results for formal and informal manufacturing sectors, respectively. The scheme of analysis is same as followed in combined manufacturing.

As conjectured, human capital proxied using literacy level is found to have significant effect on the TFPG of formal sector (row 1, Table 3.7) and no effect on the informal sector (row 1, Table 3.8). The significance level of the coefficient – be it formal or informal sector – does not change even if we control for few industries having abnormally high TFPG (Models 2). The IV estimation, however, does not change the result for formal as well as informal manufacturing sector ruling out any endogeneity concerns (Model 3).

On the basis of results, we can say that literacy has a direct impact on the TFPG of the manufacturing sector, but the impact is confined to the formal sector. This supports that there exists duality in Indian manufacturing. The presence of educated and skilled workers that matter most to the formal sector has less relevance for the informal sector as such.

3.6 Conclusions

This study examines the role of human capital as captured by literacy rate in influencing manufacturing productivity for Indian manufacturing. We examine whether the variation in TFPG for the same set of industries across Indian states and over time can be related to variations in literacy levels across these states.

A Cobb-Douglas production function is fit to the data and estimated using LP method. We estimate TFPG for nearly 90 industries for 15 major states in India for formal, informal and combined sectors using four-digit-level data. The TFPG estimates as obtained from the production function are then used to see the effect of literacy.

TFP grew steadily in the formal manufacturing sector while reported a decline in the informal manufacturing sector. We find that literacy has a crucial role to play in the TFP growth of Indian industry. We also examined whether this impact is confined to formal manufacturing firms only and found evidence in favour of it. The coefficient of literacy variable for the formal manufacturing sector is not only significant in all the variants but significantly higher than that of the coefficient for the informal manufacturing sector. On the other hand, literacy is found to have no effect on the TFPG of informal sector. Our results are robust to alternate specifications and to possible endogeneity concerns to do with the literacy measure. Our results suggest that measures should be adopted to attract a better educated and skilled workforce into the sector so as to bring about sustained increases in productivity and subsequent increase in standards of living.

One possible extension of the present chapter is to carry out analysis separately for the three categories of informal sector units – OAMEs, NDMEs and DMEs. This is because the human capital may be more relevant for DMEs which are in direct competition with small formal sector firms.

Acknowledgements This chapter forms a part of a larger study examining the effect of state-business relations on the productivity of Indian firms funded by IPPG – University of Manchester, UK (www.ippg.org.uk). We are thankful to IPPG – University of Manchester and DFID – UK for financial support. We are also thankful to the Central Statistical Organisation, for providing us access to the data, and to Nilachal Ray for his many suggestions and comments. An earlier version of this chapter looking into state-business relations on productivity was presented at the 8th International Industrial Organization conference held in Vancouver during 14–16 May 2010. The authors thank conference participants for helpful comments. The usual disclaimers apply.

References

Arnold J, Javorcik B (2005) Gifted kids or pushy parents? Foreign acquisitions and plant productivity in Indonesia. World Bank Policy Research working paper 3597

Aw BY, Roberts MJ, Winston T (2005) The complementary role of exports and R&D investments as sources of productivity growth. NBER working paper no. 11774

Bartel A, Lichtenberg F (1987) The comparative advantage of educated workers in implementing new technology. Rev Econ Stat 69:1–11

Bartelsman E, Doms M (2000) Understanding productivity: lessons from longitudinal microdata. J Econ Lit 38:569–594

Batra G, Tan H (2000) Technology and firm-size differentials in Colombia, Mexico, and Taiwan (China). World Bank Econ Rev 11:59–83

Becker GS (1964) Human capital: a theoretical and empirical analysis, with special reference to education. Princeton University Press, Princeton

Blalock G, Gertler P (2004) Learning from exporting revisited in a less developed country setting. J Dev Econ 75:397–416

Chand S, Sen K (2002) Trade liberalization and productivity growth: evidence from Indian manufacturing. Rev Dev Econ 6:120–132

Dearden L, Reed H, Van Reenen J (2000) Who gains when workers train? Training and corporate productivity in a panel of British industries. Institute for Fiscal Studies working paper W00/04

Devarajan S, Rodrik D (1991) Pro-competitive effects of trade reform: results from a CGE model of Cameroon. Eur Econ Rev 35:1157–1184

Dollar D, Hallward-Driemeier M, Mengistae T (2005) Investment climate and firm performance in developing economies. Econ Dev Cult Chang 54:1–31

Easterly W, Levine R (2001) It's not factor accumulation: stylized facts and growth models. World Bank Econ Rev 15:177–219

Fernandes AM, Isgut AE (2006) Learning-by-exporting effects: are they for real? Mimeo, The World Bank and Institute for Competitiveness & Prosperity

Goldar B, Kumari A (2003) Import liberalization and productivity growth in Indian manufacturing industries in the 1990s. Dev Econ 41:436–460

Griliches Z (1998) R&D and productivity: the econometric evidence. University of Chicago Press, Chicago

Hallward-Driemeier M, Wallsten S, Xu C (2003) The investment climate and the firm: firm-level evidence from China. World Bank, World Bank working paper 3003

Harriss RG (1999) Determinants of Canadian productivity growth: Issues and prospects. Discussion paper no. 8, Industry Canada Research Publications Programme

Hellerstein J, Neumark D (2004) Production function and wage equation estimation with heterogeneous labour: evidence from a new matched employer-employee data set, working paper no. 10325. NBER, Cambridge

Ilmakunnas P, Maliranta M, Vainionmaki J (2004) The roles of employer and employee characteristics for plant productivity. J Product Anal 21:249–276

Isaksson A (2007) Determinants of total factor productivity: a literature review. Research and Statistics Branch, UNIDO

Jones P (2001) Are educated workers really more productive? J Dev Econ 64:57–79

Kathuria V (2008) Does FDI inflow complement or substitute R&D investment by medium and high-tech firms in India? Relationship in the post-reforms period. Trans Corp 17(2):45–66

Kathuria V, Rajesh Raj SN, Sen K (2009) State business relations and manufacturing productivity growth in India, IPPG discussion paper 33. Available at www.ippg.org.uk

Kathuria V, Rajesh SNR, Sen K (2010) Organized versus unorganized manufacturing performance in the post reform period. Econ Polit Week XLV(24):55–64

Kathuria V, Rajesh Raj SN, Sen K (2011) Rain, rain, go away? The investment climate, state–business relations and firm performance in India. Int J Trade Glob Market 4(2):172–186

Kee HL (2005) Foreign ownership and firm productivity in Bangladesh garment sector. Development Research Group – Trade, The World Bank, Washington DC

Kraay A (1999) Export and economic performance: evidence from a panel of Chinese enterprises. Revue d'Economie du Developpement 1:183–207

Krugman PR, Obstfeld M (2005) International economics: theory and policy. Addison Wesley, Boston

Levinsohn J, Petrin A (2003) Estimating production functions using inputs to control for unobservables. Rev Econ Stud 70:317–342

Majumdar R (2004) Productivity growth in small enterprises: role of inputs, technological progress and 'learning by doing'. Indian J Lab Econ 47:901–911

Mazumdar D, Sarkar S (2008) Globalization labour markets and inequality in India. Routledge, New York

Melitz MJ (2003) The Impact of trade on intra-industry reallocations and aggregate industry productivity. Econometrica 71:1695–1725

Mincer J (1989) Human capital and the labour market: a review of current research. Educ Res 18:27–34

Mitra D, Ural BP (2007) Indian manufacturing: a slow sector in a rapidly growing economy. Policy Research working paper series no. 4233, The World Bank

Mukherjee D (2004) Productivity in the small manufacturing enterprises: determinants and policy issues. Indian J Lab Econ 47(4):913–927

Nicita A, Olarreaga M (2006) Trade, production, and protection, 1976–2004, Development Economics Research Group (Trade). The World Bank, Washington, DC

Nielsen H, Rosholm M (2002) Evaluation of training in African enterprises, working paper, University of Aarhus, Sweden for the Africa Region. The World Bank, Washington, DC

Raj RSN (2006) Productivity and technical efficiency in the Indian unorganized manufacturing sector: temporal and spatial analysis. Unpublished Ph.D. thesis. Department of Humanities and Social Sciences, Indian Institute of Technology Madras (IITM), Chennai

Raj RSN, Duraisamy M (2005) Structure, employment and productivity growth: evidence from the unorganized manufacturing sector in India, 1984/5-1994/5. J Int Bus Entrep 11:41–62

Rodrik D (1992) Closing the productivity gap: does trade liberalisation really help? In: Helleiner GK (ed) Trade policy, industrialisation and development: new perspectives. Clarendon, Oxford, pp 155–175

Schultz TW (1961) Investment in human capital. Am Econ Rev 51:1–17

Takii S (2003) Do education earnings differentials reflect productivity?: evidence from Indonesian manufacturing 1996, working paper 169. The European Institute of Japanese Studies, Stockholm

Tan H, Lopez-Acevedo G (2002) Mexico: in-firm training for the knowledge economy. World Bank Policy Research working paper 2957

Tybout J (2000) Manufacturing firms in developing countries: how well do they do, and why? J Econ Lit 38:11–44

Wagner J (2007) Exports and productivity: a survey of evidence from firm level data. World Econ 30:60–82

Welch F (1970) Education in production. J Polit Econ 78:35–59

Wooldridge J (1995) Introductory econometrics: a modern approach. South-Western College Publishing, Cincinnati

Chapter 4
Informality, Vulnerability and Development

Dibyendu Maiti and Arup Mitra

4.1 Introduction

Issues concerning the residual absorption of labour in the low-productivity informal sector have previously received a great deal of attention. In the present context of globalization, while most countries are aiming at maximizing growth, the issue of well-being has become increasingly important. One of the crucial dimensions of well-being is access to productive employment opportunities. Thus, the concept of pro-poor growth and various other questions relating to informalization have acquired prominence in the development literature.

Growth that is currently taking place is accompanied by informalization, for example, subcontracting in the production process and various other mechanisms that tend to leave labour with less bargaining power. On the whole, the informalization process is feared to involve substantial welfare losses and deterioration in terms of governance. There is also concern on industrialization issues, and accordingly, it has led policymakers and academicians to debate and design policies for providing a safeguard against global imbalances. It is often observed that producers engaged in small enterprises in the informal sector cater to local and regional demand. The argument usually put forward in this context is to enhance the educational level and technical skills, which in turn would promote graduation of labour to the formal sector. Keeping some of these issues in mind, this chapter makes an attempt to estimate the supply-push component of the informal sector employment across the Indian states and identifies factors that determine this supply-push informalization. In particular, this chapter examines whether education and skill development promote participation in the formal sector. Finally, we investigate whether this type of

D. Maiti • A. Mitra (✉)
Institute of Economic Growth, University of Delhi Enclave,
North Campus, Delhi 110007, India
e-mail: dibyendu@iegindia.org; arup@iegindia.org

N.S. Siddharthan and K. Narayanan (eds.), *Human Capital and Development: The Indian Experience*, DOI 10.1007/978-81-322-0857-0_4, © Springer India 2013

informalization leads to a rise in inequality in the economy and deterioration in well-being.

In the developing world, around 60–70% of the total manufacturing employment is located in the informal sector (Agenor 1996). Although a growing body of literature shows some concerns in defining the informal sector and informal entrepreneurship, a single unanimous definition has not yet emerged. However, the informal entrepreneurship, in sum, is defined as an activity or a business that is less than 42 months old and participates in the paid production and sale of goods and services that are legitimate in all respects besides the fact they are unregistered or hidden from the state to evade tax burden (Williams and Round 2007, 2008). Various approaches have explained this informal entrepreneurship from different perspectives, for example, modernization, structuralist, neo-liberal and the post-structuralist perspective. Although the size of population has been considered as a principle cause of growing informal entrepreneurship in these studies in the context of the developing world, Williams and Nadin (2010) argue that the lack in entrepreneurial spirit is perhaps more important.

An issue of concern in the present context is whether the informal sector workers are able to face the challenges of globalization. Kiso's (2008) recent work, based on three consecutive surveys (1991, 1998 and 2006) of the same sample set of textile workers in Ahmedabad, observed that more than 50%of workers were in the informal sector. Marjit et al. (2007) argued that liberal trade and investment policies may expand or contract output and employment in the informal sector. Several papers in the volume edited by Guha-Khasnobis and Kanbur (2006) analysed the state of informal enterprises in the developing world. Mitra (2004) focused on the use of informal networks, which in turn bind the informal sector workers to low-income jobs. This process restricts their upward mobility, although at the entry level, these networks play a crucial role in providing sources of livelihood.

Maiti and Marjit (2008) argue that with greater exposure to international trade, a competing export firm in the formal sector shifts much of its efforts towards marketing, leaving production activities to the informal sector. In a study based on fieldwork, Maiti (2008) further showed that the small-scale rural industries are expanding and have survived in the post-reform India in a subcontracting arrangement as a part of the production process of the relatively larger firms or traders. On the other hand, Goldar et al. (2011) argue that economic reforms have been accompanied by growing consumerism and an increasing demand of consumers for quality products. This is obviously expected to have a significantly adverse effect on the demand for the unorganized/informal sector output.

In a study of Latin American countries, Goldberg and Pavnik (2003) suggest reforms led to an increase in wage inequality and a moderate increase in income inequality in the late 1980s and early 1990s. Regardless of whether wage and income inequalities were rising or not, trade reform was accompanied by reductions in poverty, mainly through reductions in the cost of the consumption bundle of the poor and reduction in unemployment. Policies relating to the provision of education, access to credit and insurance, flexible entry and exit of firms and access to infrastructure and technical assistance can help the poor maximize the new economic opportunities offered by trade reforms.

Therefore, the role of education has appeared as one of the principal policy instruments for poverty alleviation. As the growth literature also suggests, improvements in the average education level accelerate growth through productivity enhancement and knowledge spillover. A large body of research using individual level data on education and income provides robust evidence in favour of a substantial payoff attached to investment in education (Krueger and Lindahl 2001). One corollary of this argument seems to suggest the provision of higher education would unambiguously promote growth, which will be accompanied by a shift in the workforce structure away from the informal towards the formal sector. However, it may not be a smooth process because of the segmentation of the economy. Because of the structural bottlenecks, a large component of the workforce cannot be absorbed in the formal sector, and rather, they are left in the low-cost production sector to cater to the local market. The poor cannot easily access the external market without investing in education, establishing networks and pursuing rigid registration procedures for formalization. Removal of rigid procedures and extension of subsidies and educational facilities may enable the workers to graduate from the informal to the formal sector.

This chapter is organized as follows. Section 4.2 provides the theoretical motivation. Section 4.3 presents an estimate of informal sector employment in nonagricultural activities, and based on stochastic function framework, an index of informal sector employment is worked out that can be attributed to the supply-push phenomenon. In Sect. 4.3, based on the cross-sectional variations, the important determinants of this index are identified, and we also assess the impact of supply-push informalization on inequality. Finally, in Sect. 4.4, the major findings are summarized.

4.2 Theoretical Motivation

Here, we develop a simple framework to see under what conditions education can promote participation in the formal sector. Suppose a producer in the informal sector, who is capital constrained, produces to cater to the local market. She/he manufactures certain goods to supply to the final producers, traders or directly to the consumers in the local market. Suppose the cost of manufacturing the products is cq^2 where the marginal cost is $2cq$. Here, c is a positive parameter of the marginal cost of production, and q is the output produced by the firm. The price of the goods in the local market is unity, and thereby, an informal sector producer can attain one unit value for each product sold in the local market. But, she/he can top up this value if she/he can send the products to a market outside the local area. To do so, she/he requires exposure, technical and marketing skills, a proper management education and training. The basic intuition is that if an individual gets this sort of education and training, she/he can successfully access the modern marketing network and, thus, sell to the outside market at higher prices. So, the level of education and training, denoted by e, matters for achieving a higher price of the product, that is, $\alpha(e){:}\alpha'>0$ and $\alpha'' < 0$. In other words, with a higher level of education and training, the exposure to sell the product at the national/international market would be greater. Similar specification is also available in Maiti and Marjit (2008). However, such education is not costless. Moreover, an informal sector producer cannot sell products to an outside market without proper registration and a trade license. The legal system is such that she/he would not be allowed to cater to the outside market without proper registration, which requires formal procedures involving substantial time and fees. The investment on training and registration together is assumed, for the sake of simplicity, to be A in period one, and after period one, it becomes $A(1+r)e^2$, where r is denoted as the market rate of interest. Now the profit function of the firm can be expressed as

$$\Pi(q,e) = p\alpha(e)q + (1-p)q - cq^2 - A(1+r)e^2. \qquad (4.1)$$

In the first stage, the firm takes the decision simultaneously as to whether it would produce in the formal or informal sector and what would be the optimal level of education. At the second stage, the optimum level of production will be solved. This is done using the backward induction technique.

Differentiating (4.1) with respect to q and equating to 0, we get

$$\frac{\left[p\alpha(e)+(1-p)\right]^2}{4c}.$$

Substituting for output into Π we get

$$pi(e) = \frac{\left[p\alpha(e)+(1-p)\right]^2}{4c} - A(1+r)e^2. \qquad (4.2)$$

Differentiating the above expression with respect to e, we get

$$\frac{d\Pi(e)}{de} = \frac{\left[p\alpha(e)+(1-p)\right]}{2c} \bullet p\alpha' - 2A(1+r)e = C \qquad (4.3)$$

From the above profit function, the optimum level of education can be solved. For a critical value of e, that is, $e = e^*$, we can work out the $\max \pi = \pi^*$. This is demonstrated in Fig. 4.1.

Now, if $e=0$ $\pi_0 = (1-p)^2 / 4c > 0$

In other words, the firm can earn a positive profit from the local market without having education and formal registration.

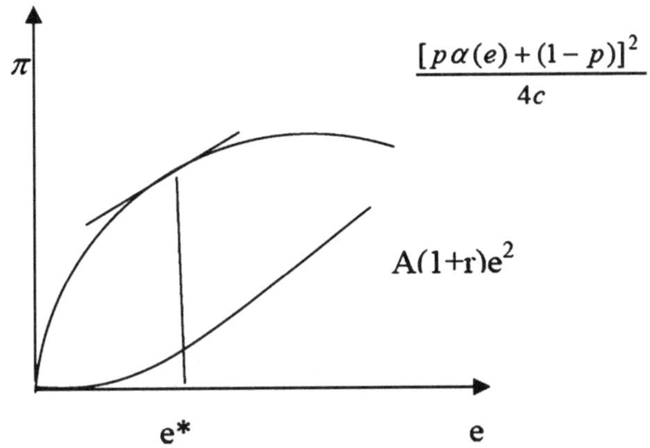

Fig. 4.1 Optimum level of education

Comparing the profit levels, π^* and π_0, the firm will decide whether formalization is beneficial or not. If $\pi_0 > \pi^*$, the firm does not want to cater to the outside market, and it remains in the informal sector. If $\pi_0 = \pi^*$, the owner of the firm remains indifferent between the level of education at 0 and e^*. But she/he prefers to opt for $e = 0$ because there is no incentive to go for higher education.

Suppose the government takes some initiative to uplift the quality of education, that is, shift the $\alpha(e)$, and reduces the costs of formalization, or ensures better transport facility (i.e. to raise p) by raising development expenditure, the profit can be raised and the aspiration for education can be enhanced.

Similarly, educational subsidy, interest subsidy, loans to firms, reduction in cost of education and formal registration (reducing A) will yield similar results. Therefore, we can infer that education may be a necessary but not sufficient condition for joining the formal sector (see Mookherjee et al. 2008). Education combined with investment in public utilities will encourage formal sector participation.

4.3 Empirical Analysis

In this section, we examine some of the implications of the theoretical construct from the empirical standpoint. Regarding the informal sector employment, the National Sample Survey Organization (NSSO) came up with estimates for nonagricultural activities, corresponding to the years 1999–2000 and 2004–2005. To derive the absolute number of workers in the informal and the formal sectors, we have adopted the following steps.

First, given the population figures from the censuses of 1991 and 2001, the average annual growth rates have been computed on the basis of which population for the year 1999–2000 and 2004–2005 has been projected. Given the NSSO estimates of worker (principal plus subsidiary) to population ratio, the absolute number of workers for these 2 years has been derived. In the next step, the NSSO estimates, of per 1,000 distribution of workers across different activities, have been applied to derive the absolute number of workers in each of the activities. In the third step, NSSO's results of the survey on the informal sector workers in nonagricultural activities have been used to split the total workers in each activity into informal and formal components. The NSSO's estimate of the per 1,000 distribution of workers in the informal sector is applied to the absolute number of workers in each activity to derive the absolute number of workers in the informal sector, which has been then deducted from the total number of workers in each activity to deduce the formal sector workers. For 1999–2000, NSSO provided the absolute number of workers in the informal sector directly. The proportions have been calculated by considering the NSSO estimate of population for the year 1999–2000. Because the NSSO's estimate of population is said to be grossly underestimated, these proportions are then applied to the absolute number of workers derived from the projected population of 1999–2000 on the basis of the decennial census figures. The adjusted set of absolute number of workers in the informal sector is then used for further analysis.

The share of the informal sector in total nonagricultural employment has been extremely large. Across states, considerable variations exist but the relative size in most of the cases is overwhelmingly large. At the all-India level, the informal sector constituted around 78%of the total nonagricultural workforce in 1999–2000 (in the rural and urban areas combined), which then increased to 84.5%in 2004–2005 (see Tables 4.1 and 4.2). This rise is evident across several states. Particularly in Maharashtra and Tamil Nadu, which are relatively industrialized states, the share increased to around 78 and 85%in 2004–2005. Given the large-scale contractualization and labour market flexibility adopted by firms in these states, the rise does not come as a surprise.

Theoretically, the informal sector can grow because of the supply-side factors and/or the demand-side factors. In the present specification, we have taken informal sector employment to be a function of certain demand-side factors approximated by the formal sector employment in various activities. Next, we pose the question—if the actual (observed) level of informal sector employment is much above the level that can be explained in terms of formal sector employment. We have analysed this in the stochastic frontier function framework. The distance of the actual informal sector employment from the level of informal sector employment, which can be explained in terms of formal sector employment, would represent the pressure of excess supplies. The higher the distance, the greater is the pressure of excess supplies of labour, leading to a residual absorption of labour in the low-productivity activities in the informal sector.

By applying the statistical stochastic frontier function framework, we can identify, based on the cross-sectional data, the extent to which different states are above the level that can be explained in terms of formal sector employment. The stochastic frontier model for informal sector employment is given by

$$\inf_i = F(\cdot)\exp\left(U_{\mathrm{i}} + V_{\mathrm{i}}\right).$$

Table 4.1 Relative employment size of the informal sector in nonagricultural activities: 1999–2000 (percent)

State	Manufacturing	Construction	Trade, hotel	Transport	Finance	Service	Aggregate
Andhra Pradesh	73.41	76.52	91.89	67.90	58.76	47.87	71.15
Arunachal Pradesh	6.34	20.45	49.86	42.07	7.42	1.41	12.89
Assam	82.26	62.96	86.42	65.85	46.22	34.46	58.51
Bihar and Jharkhand	74.93	49.02	78.29	59.53	63.10	36.04	62.57
Goa	30.48	68.71	80.08	64.13	26.81	14.63	55.82
Gujarat	73.45	69.86	91.07	67.46	56.02	25.53	67.38
Haryana	63.84	71.93	82.48	66.13	39.93	25.30	62.83
Himachal Pradesh	66.93	59.79	85.41	70.25	34.21	11.50	52.13
Jammu and Kashmir	92.17	80.41	87.92	60.30	58.34	9.47	59.41
Karnataka	76.30	71.57	86.96	66.88	46.54	27.55	67.23
Kerala	82.60	85.08	79.72	76.05	54.03	34.63	72.38
Madhya Pradesh and Chhattisgarh	71.00	53.78	90.28	66.25	54.88	26.91	62.94
Maharashtra	67.46	63.76	88.91	57.85	48.64	25.83	61.87
Manipur	90.60	91.81	87.79	79.80	34.55	12.39	54.47
Meghalaya	74.94	67.67	83.04	69.63	14.40	5.60	42.00
Mizoram	96.20	71.80	92.71	87.69	40.73	5.30	44.35
Nagaland	75.95	51.45	85.24	65.51	47.64	4.36	23.93
Orissa	83.88	60.31	89.35	57.20	47.95	33.83	68.92
Punjab	75.79	78.03	85.60	76.50	50.21	33.47	69.78
Rajasthan	85.76	76.93	93.93	73.27	54.39	28.06	72.54
Sikkim	76.50	66.59	96.63	79.74	39.68	4.66	41.24

(continued)

Table 4.1 (continued)

State	Manufacturing	Construction	Trade, hotel	Transport	Finance	Service	Aggregate
Tamil Nadu	81.47	69.75	91.09	63.66	49.69	32.08	71.60
Tripura	76.65	57.00	72.96	79.35	37.00	28.61	47.57
Uttar Pradesh and Uttaranchal	82.88	74.15	91.73	75.67	59.04	44.79	75.51
West Bengal	84.22	73.16	90.83	74.13	53.86	36.77	74.95
Andaman	68.70	49.21	77.68	40.20	67.35	13.90	45.75
Chandigarh	62.03	77.92	89.13	80.89	60.44	17.89	57.21
Dadra	65.31	30.00	101.80	94.59	132.37	29.83	66.33
Daman	44.75	84.40	98.46	68.50	45.66	44.45	62.22
Delhi	80.21	66.54	89.55	68.95	51.53	15.18	62.81
Lakshadweep	23.53	35.49	10.89	24.29	0.00	0.33	12.64
Pondicherry	68.43	69.55	91.87	83.99	67.99	26.21	68.55
All India	77.91	69.70	88.78	67.37	53.45	33.07	68.46

Source: Informal Sector in India, 1999–2000, Report No. 459(55/2.0/2), National Sample Survey Organization, Ministry of Statistics and Programme Implementation, May 2001

Note: Aggregate is the combination of all the nonagricultural activities shown in the table

Table 4.2 Relative employment size of the informal sector in nonagricultural activities: 2004–2005 (percent)

State	Manufacturing	Construction	Trade, hotel	Transport	Finance	Service	Aggregate
Andhra Pradesh	87.66	92.59	95.56	80.18	68.39	79.66	87.13
Arunachal Pradesh	43.78	4.61	47.78	64.44	18.20	29.48	30.49
Assam	84.63	72.98	88.58	74.26	55.91	53.61	73.05
Bihar	93.67	76.98	89.85	78.41	83.55	77.87	85.95
Chhattisgarh	80.16	78.96	92.91	69.51	95.39	59.50	78.08
Delhi	80.68	70.55	93.71	65.82	43.83	45.96	70.96
Goa	47.53	92.73	89.09	72.04	97.43	43.73	70.88
Gujarat	73.46	90.07	96.13	84.09	75.14	68.84	80.73
Haryana	65.54	61.35	92.12	84.41	76.65	65.77	73.73
Himachal Pradesh	59.41	45.59	92.28	56.22	76.54	55.18	60.01
Jammu and Kashmir	88.94	59.36	89.27	85.82	79.87	51.42	74.02
Jharkhand	70.18	69.96	88.43	68.29	75.59	68.83	73.88
Karnataka	87.22	85.98	95.98	83.36	52.37	68.39	83.76
Kerala	87.16	88.75	95.54	82.00	82.11	53.21	82.00
Madhya Pradesh	67.84	75.11	89.32	73.51	81.77	66.24	75.15
Maharashtra	77.14	80.16	94.51	70.24	72.29	66.10	78.49
Manipur	81.35	67.81	82.36	76.38	22.83	37.95	64.77
Meghalaya	81.35	83.12	83.08	65.77	100.00	14.31	50.56
Mizoram	87.13	56.26	80.71	77.97	63.38	34.66	55.38
Nagaland	84.28	39.99	75.70	44.23	19.98	30.94	51.99
Orissa	90.26	71.34	94.10	74.93	72.60	71.23	82.99
Punjab	88.39	86.60	95.00	78.07	93.48	56.01	82.81
Rajasthan	94.80	84.02	94.39	87.43	86.55	60.12	85.02
Sikkim	86.86	61.77	74.19	81.20	0.00	17.67	51.20
Tamil Nadu	89.40	91.11	96.88	72.32	58.42	69.94	84.92
Tripura	84.06	65.48	75.69	70.16	83.41	26.90	51.82
Uttaranchal	73.65	86.76	90.04	81.16	80.94	49.66	74.78

(continued)

Table 4.2 (continued)

State	Manufacturing	Construction	Trade, hotel	Transport	Finance	Service	Aggregate
Uttar Pradesh	88.71	84.00	93.84	77.36	83.54	76.26	86.29
West Bengal	89.22	88.35	92.98	78.00	74.77	67.92	84.19
Andaman	74.44	62.11	86.41	69.31	53.70	12.07	51.61
Chandigarh	77.92	85.83	88.55	53.60	97.50	59.44	72.67
Dadra	63.98	87.84	86.93	10.00	100.00	50.54	64.22
Daman	18.33	17.35	58.90	93.73	90.83	70.31	50.32
Lakshadweep	83.36	73.39	53.81	37.73	55.20	42.09	59.52
Pondicherry	66.87	96.86	91.65	86.59	83.45	50.22	76.77
All India	84.54	81.95	94.44	77.38	69.16	67.12	82.05

Source: Informal Sector and Conditions of Employment in India, 2004–05, Report No. 519(61/10/7), National Sample Survey Organization, Ministry of Statistics and Programme Implementation, April 2007

Note: Aggregate is the combination of all the nonagricultural activities shown in the table

Where U_i is the non-negative error measuring the distance between the frontier and the observed values and V_i is the random error. U_i captures the extent of distress-led or supply-push informalization.

The frontier-level informal sector employment is defined to be $\inf_i{}^* = F(\cdot)\exp(V_i)$. The excess informal sector employment because of the supply-side variable can be measured by the ratio of observed informal sector employment to the frontier level of employment:

$$E\inf_i = \frac{\inf_i}{\inf_i^*} = \frac{F(\cdot)\exp(U_i + V_i)}{F(\cdot)\exp(V_i)} = \exp(U_i).$$

Regarding the estimation procedure, log transformation of informal sector employment is regressed on the log transformation of various components of the formal sector employment. Cross-sectional data used for frontier function estimation requires a priori assumption regarding the one-sided distribution of the error term taken to measure the effect of supply-push phenomenon. In this case, we have assumed a half-normal distribution. The frontier equation is estimated by the maximum likelihood estimation technique.

Data from both the survey years (1999–2000 and 2000–2005) have been taken, implying we have two observations per state. Based on the magnitude of the U_i, the maximum value (indexed as 100) is chosen to represent the case with a maximum supply-push effect. Mizoram (1999–2000) corresponds to the maximum effect of excess supplies of labour. After assigning a value of 100 to Mizoram (1999–2000), other states have been indexed accordingly (Table 4.3).

4.4 Important Correlates

The next question is as follows: what determines this supply-push informal sector employment? An important determinant of labour productivity and wages in the organized industrial sector is technology. Most of the developing countries import technology from the western world because it has become cheaper to import after liberalization. UNIDO (2005) also insists that a wheel already discovered in one part of the world need not be rediscovered again by the developing world. In spite of the fact the adaptation cost of the imported technology is not negligible, the import of technology is believed to be cost-effective. However, imported technology is often capital intensive in nature because it is manufactured to suit the economic conditions of the developed countries. Being capital intensive in nature, imported technology leads to a sluggish labour absorption in the organized industrial sector with a substantive rise in labour productivity (Kato and Mitra 2008). As part of the labour productivity, growth is transferred to the workers in terms of wage increase, and this holds the possibility of widening the industrial-informal sector wage gap. With higher wage gaps, the informal sector workers may wish to withdraw and

Table 4.3 Index of distress-led or supply-push informal sector employment

State	1999–2000	2004–2005
Andhra Pradesh	53.55	94.43
Arunachal Pradesh	20.07	50.89
Assam	56.47	80.05
Bihar and Jharkhand	44.13	89.07
Goa	43.42	69.42
Gujarat	47.16	85.77
Haryana	48.8	77.95
Himachal Pradesh	47.12	51.94
Jammu and Kashmir	71.82	87.67
Karnataka	52.72	92.77
Kerala	70.2	86.41
Madhya Pradesh and Chhattisgarh	43.34	70.62
Maharashtra	34.67	67.89
Manipur	83.51	77.26
Meghalaya	61.35	
Mizoram	100	92.69
Nagaland	39.07	63.5
Orissa	59.95	93.25
Punjab	62.69	89.28
Rajasthan	69.43	99.68
Sikkim	67.09	83.76
Tamil Nadu	52.96	90.08
Tripura	73.4	68.09
Uttar Pradesh and Uttaranchal	65.51	90.65
West Bengal	62.49	88.11
Andaman	39.54	60.54
Chandigarh	73.77	79.07
Daman	75.58	82.79
Delhi	54.59	65.52
Lakshadweep	14.24	81.2
Pondicherry	87.14	94.02

Source: Authors' calculations
Note: Based on two-year panel data

strive hard to seek employment in the organized industrial sector (Mitra 1994). A similar result may also be observed if the informal sector wage rate declines in response to an increase in supply given the formal sector wage rate (Mitra 2004). Some of the informal sector workers may wish to withdraw from the labour market completely because the market wage may be substantially lower than their reservation wage. However, the possibility of observing a positive relationship between the wage gap and the informal sector employment is not ruled out because a rise in wage gap may lead to an increase in-migration, which in turn can result in a residual absorption of labour. So it would be interesting to assess which of the two mechanisms dominates or whether they neutralize each other.

One of the other determinants of productive employment is skill formation. Because direct information on skill formation is not available, education may be taken as a proxy. With higher levels of education, the quality of labour is expected to improve which, in turn, would reduce the residual absorption of labour in the informal sector. However, what we have taken in the model is only the enrolment ratio and not the number of years of education. With a rise in developmental expenditure, the quality of human capital is expected to improve, and this, in turn, would reduce the distress-led informalization. The other variable we have considered in the model relates to revenue expenditure. With greater government activities, the employment opportunities are likely to increase, which may induce migration and labour supplies. Supplies of labour, exceeding demand and/or skill mismatch, can essentially lead to supply-push growth of the informal sector. Because we have observations per state at two points of time, one time dummy has been introduced.

Revenue expenditure and development expenditure are taken as a percentage of total net state domestic product (NSDP). On the other hand, wage gap is measured as the difference between the real wage rate pertaining to the organized industry (taken from the *Annual Survey of Industries* for respective years) and the wage rate of the hired workers in the unorganized manufacturing enterprises (taken from NSSO reports on unorganized manufacturing enterprises). The nominal wages are deflated by the consumer price index for industrial workers at 1993–1994 prices. Enrolment ratio is defined as the proportion of students admitted to engineering and management studies (including all vocational institutes and ITIs) to the total number of students.

The regression results support most of the hypotheses (Table 4.4). Industrial-informal sector wage gap and developmental expenditure are seen to reduce the relative size of supply-push informal sector employment. The year dummy turns out to be significant with a positive coefficient, implying that the intercept corresponding to the second time point has been larger than the first. In fact, the relative size of the index is higher in the year 2004–2005 compared to 1999–2000 in most of the states (Table 4.3). Revenue expenditure takes a positive coefficient. The only variable not significant is the enrolment ratio. As already indicated above, this is in any case not a good proxy for skill formation. Also, in reference to the theoretical construct, it may be inferred that without improvement in the quality of education, the possibility of graduation to the formal sector does not get enhanced, and thus, the negative relationship between enrolment and informality may not turn out to be distinct.

In the next stage, we try to estimate the impact of supply-push informal sector employment on inequality and poverty. If the informalization process is demand induced, incomes in the informal sector are expected to rise, which may reduce income/expenditure inequality. On the other hand, if informalization is supply-push, inequality is expected to increase. The empirical estimate of the second equation based on the two-stage least-square technique shows a positive association between the index of supply-push informal sector employment and the Gini index of expenditure inequality. However, with poverty, there is no relationship, implying there could be many factors other than employment-related ones, which would impinge on the well-being (Table 4.4).

Table 4.4 Regression results

	Dependent variables		
Explanatory variables	INFINDEX	Gini coefficient	Poverty ratio
WAGEGAP	−0.00034**		
	(−2.33)		
DEVEXP	−2.75*		
	(−1.91)		
REVEXP	2.05*		
	(2.01)		
ENROL	0.16		
	(0.01)		
DUMMY	34.67*		
	(7.87)		
Estimated INFINDEX		0.004**	−0.053
		(6.59)	(−0.41)
INTER	53.08**	0.021	28.18**
	(3.94)	(0.44)	(2.99)
R^2	0.83	0.61	0.006
No. of observations	30	30	30

Source: DEVEXP and REVEXP are based on information given in the Handbook of Statistics on Indian Economy, Reserve Bank of India (2000 and 2005). ENROL is based on information given in the Statistical Abstract, Central Statistical Organization, Government of India (2000 and 2005). The details relating to other variables are given in the text

Note: ** and * represent significance at 5 and 10 % levels, respectively

INFINDEX index of informality, *WAGEGAP* formal and informal wage difference, *DEVEXP* share of development expenditure as percentage of NSDP, *REVEXP* share of revenue expenditure as percentage of NSDP, *ENROL* percentage of students enrolled in management and technical education, *INTER* intercept and dummy stands for year dummy

4.5 Conclusion

On the basis of National Sample Survey and population census data, this chapter has made an attempt to estimate the size of the informal sector employment in nonfarm activities across the Indian states. Using a statistical stochastic frontier function framework, first it derives the index of informal sector employment attributed to the distress-led or supply-push phenomenon. Factors that explain the interstate variations in this index include industrial-informal sector wage gap, revenue expenditure and development expenditure incurred by the government. Although skill formation is thought to be an important determinant of the quality of employment, the enrolment ratio turned out to be insignificant, possibly because the enrolment ratio is not a good proxy for skill formation. However, these results also need to be interpreted in the backdrop of the theoretical rationale provided in Sect. 4.2 of this chapter, undermining the role of education under certain conditions. Enrolment will be effective for formal sector expansion only when developmental expenditure is substantial.

Increased development expenditure is seen to bring in a decline in distress-led informalization. With improved education, health and infrastructural facilities, the employability of an individual goes up, which in turn reduces the residual type of employment. However, expansion in government activities, measured through increased revenue expenditure, raises in-migration, which in turn raises the supply-push phenomenon. We also observed that with an increase in distress-led informalization, inequality tends to rise although poverty does not show a clear-cut relationship with supply-push informalization. The rise in the wage gap between the organized or formal industrial sector and the unorganized/informal sector reduces residual-type employment as workers aspire to acquire an industrial job. Adoption of labour-intensive technology in the organized industrial sector is indeed crucial for pro-poor growth. The other policy implication is in terms of enhanced investment in the areas of human capital formation, health and physical infrastructure, encompassing the overall development of the region. Without improvement in the quality of education, the residual absorption of labour in the informal sector cannot decline.

References

Agenor P (1996) The labor market and economic adjustment. IMF Staff Pap 32:261–335

Central Statistical Organization (2000 and 2005) Statistical abstract. Ministry of Statistics and Programme Implementation, Government of India

Goldberg P, Pavnik N (2003) The response of the informal sector to trade liberalization. J Dev Econ 72(3):463–96

Goldar BN, Mitra A, Kumari A (2011) Performance of unorganized manufacturing in the post-reform period. In: Das K (ed) Micro and small enterprises in India: the era of reforms. Routledge, New Delhi

Guha-Khasnobis B, Kanbur R (2006) Informal labor markets and development. McMillan-Palgrave, Hampshire

Kato A, Mitra A (2008) Imported technology and employment: evidence from panel data on Indian manufacturing firms. In: Hashim SR, Siddharthan NS (eds) High-tech industries, employment and competitiveness. Routledge, London

Kiso J (2008) Job loss and job opportunities of factory workers in Ahmedabad flexible labor rethink. In: Sato H, Murayama M (eds) Globalisation, employment and mobility – the south Asian experience. JDE-JETRO, Japan

Krueger AB, Lindahl M (2001) Education for growth: why and for whom? J Econ Lit 35:1101–36

Maiti D (2008) Organizational morphology of rural industries and its dynamics in liberalized India. Camb J Econ 32(4):577–91

Maiti D, Marjit S (2008) Trade liberalization, production organization and informal sector of the developing countries. J Int Trade Econ Develop 17(3):453–61

Marjit S, Ghosh S, Biswas A (2007) Informality, corruption and trade reform. Eur J Polit Econ 23(3):777–89

Mitra A (1994) Urbanisation, slums, informal sector employment and poverty: an exploratory analysis. DK Publishers, Delhi

Mitra A (2004) Informal sector, networks and intra-city variations in economic activities and informal sector. Rev Reg Urban Develop Stud, Blackwell Publishing 16:2

Mookherjee D, Napel S, Ray D (2008) Aspirations, segregation and occupational choice. Boston University, Mimeo

NSSO (1999–2000) (55th Round) and (2004–2005) (61st Round) Survey of non-agricultural informal sector. Government of India, Delhi

Reserve Bank of India (2000 and 2005) Handbook of statistics on Indian economy. http://www.rbi.org.in/scripts/AnnualPublications.aspx?head=Handbook%20of%20Statistics%20on%20Indian%20Economy

UNIDO (2005) Productivity in developing countries: trends and policies. United Nations Industrial Development Organization, Vienna

Williams CC, Round J (2007) Entrepreneurship and the informal economy: a study of Ukraine's hidden enterprise culture. J Dev Entrep 12(1):119–36

Williams CC, Round J (2008) The hidden enterprise culture of Moscow: entrepreneurship and off-the-books working practices. J Dev Entrep 13(4):445–62

Williams CC, Nadin S (2010) Entrepreneurship and the informal economy: an overview. J Dev Entrep 15:361–378

Chapter 5
Labour and Energy Intensity: A Study of the Pulp and Paper Industries in India

Santosh Kumar Sahu and K. Narayanan

5.1 Introduction

The empirical research relating human capital and labour productivity has widely shown that informal interactions developing inside the firm's workforce improve the diffusion of information and foster the creation of a stock of knowledge which constitutes asset for future production processes. A number of recent studies on determinants of economic growth highlight the importance of total factor productivity (Easterly and Levine 2002) and explain that the salient features of countries' growth experience cannot be explained by factor accumulation alone. Several factors impact on changes in total factor productivity, including changes in technology and externalities, changes in the sectoral composition of production and organizational changes such as the adoption of lower cost production methods. Recently there has been increasing interest in the environmental impacts of international trade, especially in emissions embodied in trade. Instigated by globally increasing attention on climate change, energy and carbon dioxide (CO_2) emissions embodied in trade have been investigated in particular, primarily at national but also bilateral and global levels.

The developed as well as the developing countries are more worried regarding climate change as well as the energy demand issues. In December 1997, in Kyoto, the Annex-I[1] countries assumed differential commitments to reduce their greenhouse gas (GHG) emissions to an average of 5.2% below their 1990 emission rates by approximately 2010 (UNFCCC 1998). Earlier analyses of GHG

[1] Industrialized countries that are listed in Annex-I of the UN Framework Convention on Climate Change; for details, see http://www.oecd.org/document/13/0,3343,en_2649_34361_1849485_1_1_1_1,00.html

S.K. Sahu (✉) • K. Narayanan
Department of Humanities and Social Sciences, Indian Institute of Technology, Bombay, Powai, Mumbai, India
e-mail: knn@iitb.ac.in; santoshkusahu@gmail.com

N.S. Siddharthan and K. Narayanan (eds.), *Human Capital and Development: The Indian Experience*, DOI 10.1007/978-81-322-0857-0_5, © Springer India 2013

emissions have shown, however, that it will not be possible to stabilize atmospheric CO_2 concentration levels if industrialized countries alone limit their emissions (Lashof and Tirpak 1990). While the developing countries' (i.e. non-OECD countries excluding the former Soviet Union, Central and Eastern Europe) share of world fossil fuel consumption is presently small, rapid population and economic growth will result in a substantial increase of their share in the first part of the twenty-first century. Even with aggressive policies to promote energy efficiency, developing countries' energy demand is likely to grow five- to tenfold over the next 30–40 years, resulting in a threefold increase in world energy demand. Consistent with a rapid growth in energy use, carbon emissions from the developing world increased at an annual rate of 4.4% between 1990 and 1996 (Sathaye and Ravindranath 1998).

The participation of developing countries is essential for attaining the goal of global carbon abatement. Many developing countries, however, are demonstrably concerned that aggressive carbon abatement efforts on their part may have adverse effects on their economic growth and efforts to improve living standards. Hence, there is a need for enhanced analysis of their long-run energy use, carbon emission and technological trends to determine how the joint goals of economic improvement and climate protection might best be achieved. Numerous integrated assessment models (IAMs) have been developed to analyse the economic impacts of climate change (Weyant et al. 1996). Most such models show that GDP growth rates may be reduced if policies such as carbon taxes are implemented to reduce emissions. At the same time, however, most IAMs have not incorporated regional- or country-specific disaggregation. In addition, the IAM's canonical treatment of technological trends related to energy efficiency has been in terms of reduced form parameters (characteristically referred to as "*autonomous energy efficiency improvement* parameters") that do not allow for refined analysis of the relations among energy use, economic growth and policies. Consequently, an important frontier for IAM research is the simultaneous pursuit of developing country-specific analysis combined with more detailed investigation of technology, energy and productivity trends.

Following the oil shocks of the 1970s, a large body of econometric works (Roy 1992; Sarkar and Roy 1995) focused primarily on understanding short-run patterns, particularly those of inter-fuel and inter-input substitution. However, for the purpose of carbon policy, long-run trends are equally or more important. In particular, long-run patterns of technological change affecting the use of inputs, including energy, may have major consequences for estimates of the costs and benefits of various carbon policies. This fact has been the focus of considerable attention (and controversy) among energy analysts, who have focused on the magnitude and interpretation of "autonomous" trends of declining energy intensity.

In the context of human capital and increasing attention on climate policy issues, few studies have focused on relating human capital and energy consumption in industrial perspective. Therefore, this chapter is an attempt to look at this aspect for Indian industries in general and for the pulp and paper industries in particular. Labour intensity is considered as a proxy for the human capital, and energy intensity is considered as a factor showing how efficiently a firm is using the energy for its production. This study tries to focus on the following objectives:

1. Whether labour-intensive firms are also energy intensive
2. Whether substitution possibility can be established between labour and energy

This chapter uses data from the Centre for Monitoring Indian Economy (CMIE), unit-level data from 1992 to 2000. The outline of the chapter is as follows. The next section presents a brief review of literature. This section is classified in two subsections. The first subsection deals with studies dealing with productivity analysis. The second subsection deals with the studies on substitution possibilities between energy, capital and labour inputs. Section 5.3 focuses on the pulp and paper industries in Indian manufacturing industries and its current trend. Section 5.4 deals with the analysis of the data and the empirical findings, and the last section concludes the findings.

5.2 Review of Literature

There are a wide range of studies that analyse trends in total factor productivity growth in Indian industries. Most of the researchers have also focused on labour issues with capital and other factors of production. In addition to that wide range of study, it also focuses on the substitution possibility between energy, capital and labour for any industry context. The debate is based on the analyses whether energy capital and energy labour are substitutes or complementary to each other. This section tries to review the work done so far on above issues and few other studies focusing on energy- and climate-related issues. For a better understanding, we have divided this section in two subsections. The first subsection deals with the productivity studies in general and for the Indian context in particular. Consequently, studies focusing on the pulp and paper industries are also narrated. The second subsection of the study focuses on the substitution or complementarity among energy, capital and labour.

5.2.1 Studies on Productivity

In recent decades, several methodologies have been developed and applied to examine changes in productivity and technological development. A number of studies have estimated total factor productivity for the Indian economy using statistical indices within the standard growth accounting framework (Mongia and Sathaye 1998a, b; Ahluwalia 1991). Ahluwalia (1991) attempts to analyse the long-term trends in total productivity and partial productivities in the organized manufacturing sector in India from 1959–1960 to 1985–1986. The role of factor input growth and total factor productivity growth in accounting for the growth in value added is also explored. The analysis is conducted at a detailed level of disaggregation for 63 constituent industry groups at 3-digit level as well as for the four use-based sectors of manufacturing, i.e. intermediate goods, consumer nondurables, consumer durables and capital goods.

For as many as 36 industries accounting for over 50% of the total value added in manufacturing in 1970–1971, however, the contribution of total factor productivity growth was found negative. The focus was more on these industries: food manufacturing except sugar, iron and steel and nonferrous metals. For almost all of the 63 industries, capital intensity showed a strong and significant positive growth. There were a few industries which even experienced a decline in labour productivity.

Study by Pradhan and Barik (1999) attempts to find a solution by considering TFPG as a result of interaction between economies of scale and technical change. Thus, it seeks to lay emphasis on proper management of scale economies and technical change for producing a desired TFPG. For that purpose, estimation of TFPG is carried out with the help of translog cost function, which gives information on these two components simultaneously. The empirical findings of the exercise on data of aggregate manufacturing sector and eight selected industries of India indicate that both scale economies and technical change have registered a declining trend in recent years in the process of a declining TFPG.

Roy et al. (1999) reported productivity growth and input trends in six energy-intensive sectors of the Indian economy using growth accounting and econometric methods. The econometric work estimates rate and factor price biases of technological change using a translog production model with an explicit relationship defined for technological change. Estimates of own-price responses indicated that raising energy prices would be an effective carbon abatement policy for India. The study provides information relevant for the analysis of costs and benefits of carbon abatement policies applied to India and thus contributes to the emerging body of modelling and analysis of global climate policy.

Schumacher and Sathaye (1999) derive both statistical and econometric estimates of productivity growth for the pulp and paper industries in India. Using translog specification, they reveal that technical progress in India's pulp and paper sector has been biased towards the use of energy and material, while it has been capital and labour saving. The decline in productivity was caused largely by the protection afforded by high tariffs on imported paper products and other policies, which allowed inefficient, small plants to enter the market and flourish. To verify whether these trends will continue into the future, particularly where energy use is concerned, they examined the current changes in structure and energy efficiency undergoing in the sector. Their analysis shows that with liberalization and tighter environmental controls, this industry is moving towards higher efficiency and productivity.

Goldar (2000) found that the growth rate in employment in the organized manufacturing sector in India for the period 1990–1991 to 1997–1998 was 2.69% per annum which was well above the growth rate of 0.53% per annum achieved in the 1980s. He attributed two major reasons for this growth in employment: slowdown in growth of real wages in the 1990s and faster growth of small- and medium-sized factories in organized manufacturing, which are more labour intensive as compared to large-sized factories. He also highlighted that the increase in employment in the organized manufacturing sector which took place in the 1990s was accounted for by private-sector factories.

Assuming a translog specification of four inputs (KLEM) for production function, Mongia et al. (2001) use growth accounting to decompose growth of output into growth of inputs and residual representing the total factor productivity growth. The major finding of the chapter is that overall productivity growth in these industries was quite low during 1973–1994. However, there was significant difference in productivity growth across these industries during this same time. These differences can to a large extent be explained by the nature and timing of policy changes in individual sectors. The total factor productivity growth was significantly positive for fertilizer industry, positive but low in case of aluminium and cement industries and negative for the iron and steel and paper industries. The analysis of two subperiods, 1973–1981 and 1981–1994, showed that changes in technologies and production conditions triggered or induced by policy reforms helped increase productivity growth significantly in the cement and the fertilizer industry. The effect of policy changes was less significant in the case of aluminium because of lumpiness of investment and because of the inherent nature of the technology. However, the removal of market constraints and the addition of a modern plant did raise the growth rate in the second subperiod significantly. Productivity growth was adversely affected in the case of iron and steel and paper, where due to lack of a clear long-term perspective, the positive effects of policy reforms were overwhelmed by institutional and market conditions, at least temporarily. Finally, overall policy reforms did not go far enough to significantly affect productivity growth in India's energy-intensive manufacturing sectors.

Chaudhuri (2002) studied the changes in labour intensity for 3-digit groups in the organized manufacturing sector for 1990–1991 and 1997–1998. He found that labour intensity had progressively gone down from 0.78 in 1990–1991 to 0.56 in 1997–1998. Uma and Unni (2004) observed a sharp growth in capital intensity and declining labour intensity in both organized and unorganized sectors. The positive growth in capital intensity was not accompanied by a rise in capital productivity in both sectors, which again implied a substitution of capital for labour, without any technological upgradation, across all industry groups at the 2-digit level in both the sectors. Nagaraj (2004) pointed out that faster employment generation in organized manufacturing was restricted mainly to the first half of the 1990s. As the boom went bust, there was a steep fall in employment in the second half of the 1990s. Relative cost of labour did not seem to matter in employment decisions, as the wage:rental ratio declined secularly. According to him, about 1.1 million workers, or 15% of the workers in the organized manufacturing sector in the country, lost their jobs between 1995–1996 and 2000–2001.

In a study, Das et al. (2009) attempted to identify and examine labour-intensive industries in the organized manufacturing sector in India in order to understand their employment generation potential. Using the data from the Annual Survey of Industries, the labour intensity for 97 industries at the 4-digit disaggregate level was computed for the period 1990–1991 to 2003–2004. The study identifies 31 industries as "labour-intensive industries" within India's organized manufacturing sector. The study found that labour intensity has declined not only for capital-intensive industries but also for labour-intensive industries during the selected time period.

The increase in output failed to generate enough employment growth resulting in a significant decline in employment elasticity. The chapter briefly highlights the plausible factors that could have had an impact on labour intensity as well as on the performance of the organized manufacturing sector over the study period.

5.2.2 Studies on Energy Substitution

Estimates of energy substitution are sensitive to the industries and regions of study. The economics of substitution is based on the microeconomics of production. Allen (1938) remains a fundamental source along with Varian (1984) and Takayama (1993). Cameron and Schwartz (1980) and Denny et al. (1981) find differences in estimated energy substitution across industries and countries. Caloghiro et al. (1997) find electricity a weak substitute for capital and labour in Greek manufacturing during the 1980s, implying electricity subsidies lowered the demand for capital and labour. Barnett et al. (1998) show that electricity is a weak substitute for both capital and labour in major Alabama industries and note that regulatory constraints are binding due to inelastic electricity demand. Mahmud (2000) finds very little substitution between energy and other inputs but weak substitution between electricity and gas in Pakistan manufacturing.

There has also been a considerable amount of econometric work on inter-fuel and inter-input substitution for Indian economy (Ganguli and Roy 1995) but very little (Jha et al. 1993) on long-run trends in the relations between technological change and fuel or input substitution. A comprehensive survey of research on total factor productivity in East Asia reveals a focus on capital and labour inputs, rather than energy (Felipe 1997). The standard growth accounting approach, pioneered by Solow (1957) and further developed by Denison (1974, 1979, 1985), can be employed to study long-run trends in energy use and its relationship to other economic variables. In addition, Christensen et al. (1971), Hudson and Jorgenson (1974), Jorgenson and Fraumeni (1981), Jorgenson et al. (1987) and Hogan and Jorgenson (1991) have developed and applied methods that allow for enhanced analysis of relationship between substitution effects induced by changes in relative factor prices and "pure productivity" trends, on a sector-specific basis over long time. They have demonstrated that combining a finer level of analysis (in particular sectoral disaggregation) with a form of endogeneity in the modelling of technological change can reveal patterns that are not readily detected by more traditional methods.

Chang (1994) finds little difference between translog and constant elasticity production functions in Taiwanese manufacturing and reports that energy and capital are substitutes. Yi (2000) finds substitution varies across translog and Leontief production functions in Swedish manufacturing industries. According to Li et al. (2004), the performance of the pulp and paper industries is mostly dependent on the size and age of the firms. As the size and age of the firm grows, they become more productive. Based on the analysis on the US paper mills, they found that the growth of pulp and paper mills in the USA from 1970 to 2000 depended mostly on size and age of the firms. Firms grew according to Gibrat's law, and post-1970 mills grew faster than pre-1971 firms. Firms stopped growing at approximately 22 years of age. But most firms survived beyond that; thus, growth was not necessary for survival but characteristic of the early phase of the firm life cycle. Less integrated firms grew slower, so did more specialized firms. Firm location was uncorrelated with growth, but location mattered indirectly by facilitating or hindering firm with growth-conducive characteristics.

Hseu and Shang (2005) measure the productivity of the pulp and paper industries in OECD countries from 1991 to 2000. They calculated the Malmquist productivity index by using nonparametric-frontier approach and decomposed in two components: "technical change" and "efficiency change". Their results showed that the productivity change of the pulp and paper industries in OECD countries ranged from Switzerland's 0.9% to Japan's 2.4% over the sample period. The Nordic nations (Finland, Norway and Sweden) recorded 1.2–1.5% improvement in their performance, and the productivity of the Canadian pulp and paper industries increased by 2%.

Doonan et al. (2005) examined the role of communities to create incentives for local industrial facilities to reduce their pollution. They found that firms face both internal and external pressures to improve their environmental performance. Using primary data collected for 750 Canadian pulp and paper industries during 1992, they further found that the government policies are much of a barrier for the Canadian pulp and paper industries. However, financial and consumer markets are not most important barriers. They found that education status of employee is one of the important determinants of environmental performance. The regulatory intervention is also found as the major determinants of environmental performance of the pulp and paper industries. Unlike other industrial sectors, the pulp and paper industries produce energy as by-products.

Balasubrahmanya (2006) probes the role of labour efficiency in promoting energy efficiency and economic performance with reference to small-scale brick enterprises' cluster in an Indian state. He narrates that in brick industries, the technology in use being similar, labour efficiency has a negative influence on energy cost. Therefore, those enterprises that exhibited higher labour productivities had lower average energy intensity and higher returns to scale as compared to those that had lower labour productivities. Considering this improvement of labour efficiency can be an alternative approach for energy efficiency improvement in energy-intensive small-scale industries in developing countries like India, which face the obstacle of financial constraints in upgrading technology as a means of energy efficiency improvement. Since labour productivity had a negative influence on energy cost, he grouped the brick enterprises into two groups based on their average labour productivity. He found that the two groups differed in terms of other economic ratios such as capital intensity, capital productivity, energy intensity and value-added share in the value of output.

Ma et al. (2009) measure technological change, factor demand, inter-factor and inter-fuel substitutability for China. They use individual fuel price data and employ two-stage approach to estimate total factor cost functions and fuel-share equations.

Both inter-factor and inter-fuel substitution elasticities are calculated, and the change in energy intensity is decomposed. Their results suggest that energy is substitutable for capital regionally and for labour nationally. Capital substitutes for energy more easily than labour does. Energy intensity changes vary by region, but the major drivers seem to be "budget effect" and "adoption of energy-intensive technologies", which might be embodied in high-level energy-using exports and sectors. They conclude that, after decomposing energy intensity, the "budget effect" and "technological changes" are the two major driving forces of the changes in energy intensity nationally. The variations in "budget effect" across regions are most likely related to the differences in regional economic growth and industrial structure. Further, they find that the technological changes or innovative activities can be embodied in capital investment, equipped labour, export goods and even sectoral shifts. In addition to the above studies, an issue of research interest has been the impact of various monitoring and enforcement actions undertaken by environmental regulators. A number of authors have examined whether or not the public disclosure of environmental performance may create incentives for pollution control (Foulon et al. 2002; Cohen 1998; World Bank 2000).

Based on the above discussion on studies in the manufacturing industries in general and the pulp and paper industries in particular for India, we can observe that most of the research works, except Balasubrahmanya (2006), have not explicitly tried to focus on the relationship between labour intensity and energy intensity. Therefore, this chapter intends to fill this research gap. Both the issues are of importance for an emerging economy like India. As the pulp and paper industries in India are one of the highly energy-consuming industries in the manufacturing sector, we have tried to establish relationship between labour and energy intensity using unit-level data. The next section of the chapter focuses on a brief introduction and the current state of the pulp and paper industries in India.

5.3 The Pulp and Paper Industry in India

The first paper mill in India was set up at Sreerampur, West Bengal, in 1812. However, large-scale mechanized technology of papermaking was introduced in early 1905. Since then, the raw material for the paper industry underwent a number of changes, and over a period of time, besides wood and bamboo, other nonconventional raw materials have been developed for use in the papermaking. The paper industry is categorized as forest-based and agro-based and others (waste paper, secondary fibre, bast fibres and market pulp). Currently, the pulp and paper industry in India is the 15th largest paper industry in the world.

Indian paper industry has been de-licensed under the Industries Development and Regulation Act (1951) with effect from 1997. Foreign direct investment (FDI) up to 100% is allowed on automatic route on all activities except those requiring industrial licenses where prior governmental approval is required. The installed capacities of Indian pulp and paper mills vary over a wide range of 5 ton per day to 600 ton per day. Indian paper mills are categorized into (1) large mills with installed

Table 5.1 Share of different indicators of the pulp and paper industries as compared to Indian manufacturing industries (in percent)

Year	Units[a]	Fixed capital	Workers	Wages
2007	2.80	2.59	2.55	2.04
2006	2.67	2.44	1.91	1.98
2005	2.67	2.46	1.94	2.17
2004	2.76	2.53	2.09	2.30
2003	2.77	2.66	2.25	2.38
2002	2.72	3.30	2.20	2.31
2001	2.63	2.69	2.21	2.48
Growth rate (pulp and paper industries)	1.16	0.99	0.88	0.93
Growth rate (manufacturing industries)	1.46	1.04	1.26	1.04

Source: Researchers' calculation based on data from the "Principal Characteristics by Major Industry Group", ASI, various years, MOSPI, GoI

[a]Number of pulp and paper units to total manufacturing industries

capacity of more than 100 ton per day and (2) small mills with capacity less than 100 ton per day. The small units account for more than 50% production capacity and characterized by poor energy efficiency. About 80–85% of energy is used for process heating, while the share of electricity accounts for 15–20%. More than 80% of electricity used in large wood-based mills is met by cogeneration units.

Growth of paper industry in India has been constrained due to high cost of raw materials, power cost and geographically concentration of mills. Government has taken several policy measures to remove the bottlenecks of availability of raw materials and infrastructure development. For instance, to overcome short supply of raw materials, duty on pulp and waste paper and wood logs/chips has been reduced. As of 2007–2008, the Indian paper industry has a total turnover of more than Rs. 10,000 crore and provides direct employment to 200,000 people and indirectly to another 100,000 persons. Despite low per capita consumption of paper and paperboards, the industry has made a steady progress in the last five decades. At present, about 60.8% of the total production is based on non-wood raw material and 39.2% on wood. Import of paper and paper products have been growing over the years. The imports during 2000–2001 were to the tune of 0.152 million metric tons. The domestic demand for newsprint is met partly from indigenous production and partly by import. The demand of paper and paper products in India has continuously been increasing over the time. However, per capita paper consumption in India is about 5.5 kg in the year 2003 as against world average of 50 kg.

Table 5.1 gives a profile of the pulp and paper industries in comparison to the Indian manufacturing industries from 2001 to 2007. The data is drawn from the principle characteristics by major industry group published by the Annual Survey of Industries. In 2001, the share of the pulp and paper industries to manufacturing industries was 2.63% which increased to 2.80% in 2007. The growth in number of firms for manufacturing industries is found to be 1.46% from 2001 to 2007, and growth of number of firms in the pulp and paper industries is calculated to be 1.16%.

Therefore, growth in number of firms for total manufacturing industries is found higher than the growth in number of firms in the pulp and paper industries in India from 2001 to 2007. The pulp and paper industries hold 2.69% of fixed capital in manufacturing industries in 2001. The share went up to 3.30% in 2002, and in the subsequent years till 2007, the share of fixed capital started decreasing, and in 2007, the share was found to be 2.59% of the total manufacturing industries. The growth of fixed capital was calculated at 1.04% for the Indian manufacturing; however, the growth in the fixed capital for the pulp and paper industries was calculated to be at 0.99% for 2001 to 2007. Hence, growth in the fixed capital for the pulp and paper industries is also found less than the growth in the manufacturing industries. The percentage share of number of employees in the pulp and paper industries increased from 2.21% in 2001 to 2.55% in 2007. The growth of employees in the pulp and paper industries increased at 0.88% from 2001 to 2007. However, at the same time, the wages paid to the workers as a share of the total wages paid to the manufacturing industries have declined from 2.48% in 2001 to 2.04% in 2007. With this brief profile of the pulp and paper industries in Indian manufacturing industries, the next section is focused on the data sources, methodology and analysis.

5.4 Data, Methodology and Analysis

Energy intensity is one of the important areas of studies for economists as well as climate scientists. For Indian case, we can find very few works dealing with the energy intensity at the firm level. In an earlier attempt, Kumar (2003), Sahu and Narayanan (2011), Sahu and Narayanan (2010) and Goldar (2010) have tried to study factors affecting the energy intensity at firm level for Indian manufacturing using the structure-conduct-performance approach. They found that labour, capital, age of the firm, MNE affiliation of the firm and R&D expenditures are the major determinants of energy intensity for Indian manufacturing industries. This study follows a similar approach to look at the relationship between the labour and energy intensity for the pulp and paper industries in Indian manufacturing industries. Labour intensity is a crucial issue in linking the energy intensity as it gives the complementarities or substitution possibility between labour and energy. As stated earlier, there are wide range of studies focusing on the substitution possibility between energy, capital and labour. For instance, Ma et al. (2009) studied the Chinese economy on the substitution possibility and found that energy substitutes for capital at the regional level and labour substitutes for the national level. However, overall he found that capital substitutes more easily than labour does. This study focuses on energy and labour intensity and uses few firm-specific characteristics to find the relationship between labour and energy intensity. The definitions of variables constructed are given in Table 5.2.

Data used in this study are collected from the Centre for Monitoring Indian Economy (CMIE PROWESS Electronic) database. The downloaded data consists of 2075 observations however, after cleaning 1949 observations left for the analysis which makes an unbalanced panel from 1992 to 2009. Based on the economic

Table 5.2 Definition of variables

Sl. no	Variable	Symbol used	Definition
1.	Energy intensity	EI	The ratio of expenses on energy consumption to sales
2.	Capital intensity	CI	The ratio of total capital employed to total value of the output
3.	Labour intensity	WI	Ratio of wages and salaries to sales
4.	Profit intensity	PI	Profit after sales as a ratio to sales
5.	Age	AGE	As a measure of age, we subtract the year of incorporation from the year of the study
6.	Size	SIZE	Size of the firm is measured by log of sales
7.	Research intensity	RI	R&D intensity is measured as ratio of R&D expenses to sales
8.	Technology import intensity	ETI	Expenditure on import of capital goods/sales turnover of the firm
9.	Industry dummy	MNE	This dummy takes the value 1 for the foreign-owned firms and 0 for the rest
10.	BSE dummy	BSE	This dummy takes the value 1 for the BSE-registered firms and 0 for the rest

activity classification as classified in the CMIE, we have classified the firms in five different groups. The five major classifications are (1) paper, paperboard; (2) newsprint; (3) kraft paper; (4) paper tarred, plastic coated; and (5) paper and paperboard, corrugated, creped, embossed. Further, we have classified the sample based on listed and non-listed and ownership (domestic and foreign) status.

From Table 5.3, it is clear that the first group of the firms (paper, paperboard firms) represents only domestic firms as in this list of firms there are no foreign firms in the data set. We can see that the energy intensity is higher for the firms that are listed (0.16) as compared to the non-listed domestic firms. However, the labour intensity is found higher for the non-listed firms (0.26) as compared to the listed domestic firms (0.06). In case of capital intensity, we found that the domestic non-listed firms are higher capital intensive. In this classification, we can observe that the domestic-listed firms are lesser labour intensive and higher energy intensive. For the economic activity group 2 (newsprint firms), we can see that there are four classifications: the non-listed domestic and foreign firms as well as the listed domestic and foreign firms. In this classification, we can observe that energy intensity is higher for the listed foreign firms as compared to the other three categories and found to be least for firms that are listed and domestic firms. In case of the labour intensity, we can observe that the listed foreign firms are higher labour-intensive and the non-listed domestic firms are less labour intensive. However, for capital intensity, listed domestic firms are higher capital intensive and non-listed foreign firms are the least capital intensive. Therefore, we can summarize that the listed foreign firms that fall in this category are higher energy intensive and higher labour

Table 5.3 Energy intensity, labour intensity and capital intensity based on grouping of different firm-specific characteristics

		Energy intensity	Labour intensity	Capital intensity
(1) Paper, Paperboard				
Domestic firms	Non-listed	0.126	0.260	1.650
	Listed	0.163	0.064	1.057
Foreign firms	Non-listed	NA	NA	NA
	Listed	NA	NA	NA
(2) Newsprint				
Domestic firms	Non-listed	0.178	0.055	1.270
	Listed	0.175	0.074	2.369
Foreign firms	Non-listed	0.187	0.064	0.825
	Listed	0.217	0.087	0.909
(3) Kraft paper				
Domestic firms	Non-listed	0.176	0.452	5.755
	Listed	0.225	0.166	12.677
Foreign firms	Non-listed	0.187	0.072	0.604
	Listed	0.130	0.078	0.417
(4) Paper tarred, plastic coated				
Domestic firms	Non-listed	0.148	0.110	1.675
	Listed	0.183	0.066	1.258
Foreign firms	Non-listed	NA	NA	NA
	Listed	NA	NA	NA
(5) Paper and paperboard, corrugated, creped, embossed				
Domestic firms	Non-listed	0.208	0.645	16.082
	Listed	0.193	0.079	2.029
Foreign firms	Non-listed	0.190	0.081	0.831
	Listed	NA	NA	NA

Source: Researchers' calculation based on data from CMIE

intensive too. In the case of economic activity group 3 (kraft paper firms), we can observe that listed domestic firms are higher energy intensive as compared to the other classifications, and the least energy intensive are the listed foreign firms. In case of the labour intensity, we can see that the non-listed domestic firms are higher labour-intensive and the non-listed foreign firms are the least labour intensive. The listed domestic firms are found to be higher capital intensive and the listed foreign firms are found to be least capital intensive.

In case of the fourth classification (paper tarred, plastic coated firms), we can find only two sub-classifications: the non-listed domestic firms and the listed domestic firms. Among these two calcifications, we can see that the listed domestic firms are higher energy intensive and the non-listed domestic firms are the higher labour intensive. In case of the capital intensity, we can see that the non-listed domestic firms are higher capital intensive (1.67) as compared to the listed domestic firms (1.25). The economic activity group five (paper and paperboard, corrugated, creped, embossed firms) comprises three sub-classifications: non-listed domestic firms, non-listed foreign firms and listed domestic firms. From Table 5.3, it is evident that

Table 5.4 Energy, labour and capital intensity based on each economic group

Economic activity group	Energy intensity	Labour intensity	Capital intensity
(1) Paper, paperboard	0.145	0.160	1.347
(2) Newsprint	0.180	0.063	1.592
(3) Kraft paper	0.192	0.315	8.999
(4) Paper tarred, plastic coated	0.165	0.088	1.472
(5) Paper and paperboard, corrugated, creped, embossed	0.201	0.373	9.330
Full sample	0.195	0.299	8.146

Source: Researchers' calculation based on data from CMIE

the energy intensity is higher for the non-listed domestic firms and least for the non-listed foreign firms. In case of the labour intensity, we can see that the non-listed domestic firms are higher labour intensive and the listed domestic firms are the least labour intensive. However, capital intensity is highest for the firms that are non-listed domestic and least for the firms that are non-listed foreign.

Based on the five economic activity classifications, we can observe that firms listed in group 5 are the energy-intensive group and group 1 the least energy-intensive ones. In case of the labour intensity, we can see that paper and paperboard, corrugated, creped, embossed firms are labour intensive and newsprint firms are the least labour intensive. In case of the capital intensity, we can observe that the paper and paperboard, corrugated, creped, embossed firms are the capital intensive and paper, paperboard are the least capital intensive. In comparison to the mean energy intensity of the sample, we can observe that four groups (1, 2, 3 and 4) are less energy intensive and the 5th group of the pulp and paper industries is higher energy intensive. In case of the labour intensity, we can observe that two groups (3 and 5) are higher energy labour intensive as compared to the mean labour intensity of the full sample. The result for the capital intensity is also same as groups 3 and 5 that are higher capital intensive as compared to the mean capital intensity of the full sample (see Fig. 5.1 for details) (Table 5.4).

We have further classified the sample in two major groups based on the BSE listing. We can see that the non-listed firms are less energy intensive as compared to the listed firms. In this case, we can also see that the non-listed firms are lesser energy intensive as compared to the mean energy consumption of the full sample. In labour intensity front, we can see that the non-listed firms are higher labour intensive as compared to the listed firms (Table 5.5). Further, the listed firms are higher capital intensive as compared to the non-listed firms. From Table 5.6, we can observe that energy intensity is higher for the domestic firms and less for the foreign-owned firms. However, the energy intensity for the domestic firm and the full sample is much nearer. Looking at the labour intensity, we can observe that the labour intensity is higher for domestic firms as compared to the foreign firms, which is even higher as compared to the full sample. We found the domestic firms to be more capital intensive as compared to the foreign firms.

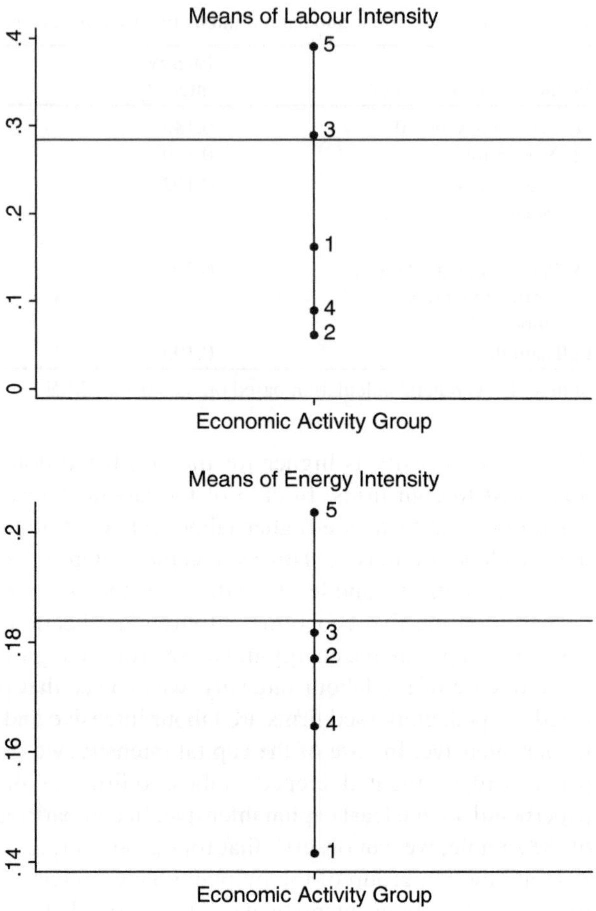

Fig. 5.1 Classification of labour and energy intensity for different industry subgroups

Table 5.5 Energy, labour and capital intensity based on BSE listing of firms

Classification based on listing of firms	Energy intensity	Labour intensity	Capital intensity
BSE non-listed firms	0.180	0.442	7.115
BSE-listed firms	0.213	0.138	9.307
Full sample	0.195	0.299	8.146

Source: Researchers' calculation based on data from CMIE

Further, the analysis of energy, labour and capital intensity for full sample of the pulp and paper industries is carried out to observe the changing patterns of the parameters over the period of time. In case of energy intensity, we can see that in 1994, the industry has recorded least energy intensity, followed by most recently in 2009. However, during 1995, the industries have recorded the highest level of energy intensity, followed by 2005. In case of labour intensity, we can see that the labour

Table 5.6 Energy, labour and capital intensity based on ownership of firm

Ownership group	Energy intensity	Labour intensity	Capital intensity
Domestic firms	0.195	0.301	8.218
Foreign firms	0.188	0.074	0.747
Total	0.194	0.299	8.146

Source: Researchers' calculation based on data from CMIE

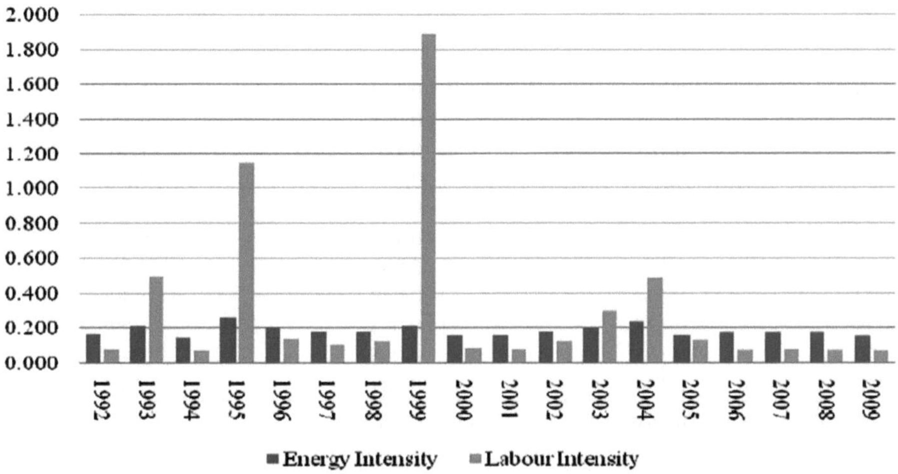

Fig. 5.2 Comparison of energy and labour intensity from 1992 to 2009

intensity recorded highest in 1995. However, in 1994, the industries have recorded the least labour intensity. In 1992, the pulp and paper industries have recorded the least capital intensity. The highest capital intensity can be seen for the year 1999. Figure 5.2 represents the changes in labour intensity and energy intensity over period of time. Except for the years 1993, 1995, 1999, 2003 and 2004, the labour intensity of the sample is lower than that of the energy intensity. For all other years, the energy intensity is higher when compared to the labour intensity (Table 5.7).

Figure 5.3 gives the growth rates of energy and labour intensity for the pulp and paper industries in three different periods. The total period of the study is from 1992 to 2009, and the first subperiod is from 1992 to 2000 and the second subperiod is from 2000 to 2009. We can see from the figure that the growth in energy intensity from 1992 to 2000 and from 2000 to 2009 is higher than that of labour intensity. However, the growth in the first period is little higher than that of the second period. However, when we consider the full time period, we can see that the growth in labour intensity is much higher than that of energy intensity. To check whether the labour-intensive industries are also highly energy intensive, we have cross-tabulated energy and labour intensity of the full sample. The labour intensity is classified into four major groups from 1 to 4, where group one represents the least labour-intensive firms and group four stands for higher labour-intensive firms. The mean energy intensity of the firms falling in each of the categories is given in Table 5.8.

Table 5.7 Energy, labour and capital intensity changes from 1992 to 2009

Year	Energy intensity	Labour intensity	Capital intensity
1992	0.163	0.076	0.933
1993	0.210	0.493	4.149
1994	0.140	0.065	1.439
1995	0.257	1.149	7.378
1996	0.206	0.139	1.820
1997	0.184	0.106	1.886
1998	0.182	0.121	4.213
1999	0.207	1.891	31.440
2000	0.160	0.084	1.320
2001	0.158	0.075	3.159
2002	0.181	0.120	1.905
2003	0.196	0.294	7.543
2004	0.235	0.488	13.499
2005	0.162	0.124	10.323
2006	0.179	0.071	1.590
2007	0.174	0.079	5.406
2008	0.178	0.073	1.598
2009	0.153	0.065	1.430
1992–2009	0.184	0.284	5.881

Source: Researchers' calculation based on data from CMIE

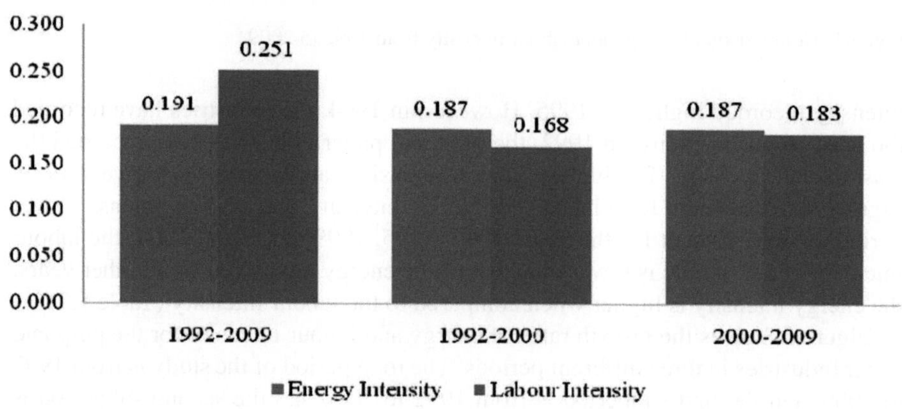

Fig. 5.3 Annual growth in energy and labour intensity for various time periods

From Table 5.8, it is clear that firms with less labour intensity are more energy intensive as compared to group 2 which is higher labour intensive. Further, we can observe that labour-intensive firms are falling in group 4. Except for group 3, we can see that in all other groups where there is an increase in the labour intensity, the energy intensity has also increased. However, the phenomenon is not clear from the above cross-tabulation. Therefore, we have utilized an econometric specification to capture this phenomenon. In the econometric investigation, we have tried to look at

Table 5.8 Classification of energy intensity based on labour intensity categories

Labour intensity group	Energy intensity	Labour intensity
1	0.165	0–0.25
2	0.158	0.25–0.50
3	0.184	0.50–0.75
4	0.229	0.75–0.99

Source: Researchers' calculation based on data from CMIE

the energy intensity change that is explained by the other factors of production. To make the argument more focused, we have also used other factors of production at the firm level, which are the structure, conduct and performance variables of the firm. Here we consider the labour intensity as the proxy for the human capital of the firm and energy intensity as the proxy for better performance of the firms. As stated earlier, we have used the unbalanced panel data of the pulp and paper industries from 1992 to 2009. Initially after getting the descriptive statistics and the correlation matrix of the variables, we have estimated using OLS. Further, fixed and random effect models are being used for better explanation. The functional form of the econometric specification takes the following:

$$EI_{it} = \alpha + \beta_1 CI_{it} + \beta_2 LI_{it} + \beta_3 LI_{it} + \beta_4 AGE_{it} + \beta_5 SIZE_{it} + \beta_6 PI_{it} + \beta_7 TI_{it} + \beta_8 RD_{it} + \beta_9 BSE_{it} + \beta_{10} MNE_{it} + \beta_{11} LID_{it} + u_{it} \quad (5.1)$$

This specification follows earlier work done by Sahu and Narayanan (2010) and Goldar (2010). To avoid possible *heteroskedasticity*, we have defined the size as natural logarithmic of net sales. Further, to check the nonlinearity between labour and energy intensity, we have estimated with square of labour intensity in Equation 5.1. The definitions of these variables are given in Table 5.2.

The descriptive statistics of the sample is given in Table 5.9. We can observe that the mean energy intensity is 0.19, with a standard deviation of 0.60 and the minimum energy intensity 0.001 and maximum at 25.0. In case of labour intensity, the mean is calculated at 0.299 where the minimum labour intensity is at 0.003 and the maximum labour intensity is found at 185 and the mean capital intensity of the full sample of 1949 firms are found to be 8.14.

The correlation matrix of variables of interest is given in Table 5.10. From the correlation analysis, we can see that energy intensity has a positive relationship with labour, capital and size of the firm. However, correlation coefficient is found higher in case of energy intensity and capital intensity. On the other hand, we can see that technology intensity, profit intensity and age of the firm are found to be negatively related to energy intensity. In case of labour intensity, we can see that energy intensity, capital intensity and size of the firm are found to be positively related and all other variables are negatively related. However, in this case also, the capital intensity of the firms is found to be having higher correlation coefficient. The Hausman test statistics comparing the estimates of fixed and random effects suggests that the random effect model is a better explanation of the model as compared to the fixed

Table 5.9 Descriptive statistics of the full sample

Variable	Mean	Std. dev.	Min	Max
EI	0.196	0.604	0.001	25.000
LI	0.299	4.822	0.003	185.000
CI	8.147	135.843	0.000	5,205.000
TI	0.568	0.222	0.000	6.000
PI	−1.073	16.744	−500.000	21.164
Size	3.271	1.512	−3.507	7.782
Age	18.840	13.490	1.000	106.000
RD	0.000	0.003	0.000	0.067
Observations	1,949			

Source: Researchers' calculation based on data from CMIE

Table 5.10 Correlation matrix

Variables	EI	LI	CI	TI	PI	Size	Age	RD
EI	1.000							
LI	0.423	1.000						
CI	0.860	0.641	1.000					
TI	−0.115	−0.112	−0.107	1.000				
PI	−0.368	−0.907	−0.513	0.116	1.000			
Size	0.016	0.055	0.036	−0.022	−0.052	1.000		
Age	−0.038	−0.031	−0.032	0.000	0.035	0.010	1.000	
RD	−0.001	−0.005	−0.005	−0.006	0.006	0.079	−0.052	1.000

Source: Researchers' calculation based on data from CMIE

effect model. Hence, the result of random effect model is explained here. In the data set, the firm-specific variable is considered as the panel proxy, and year is considered as the time variable; therefore, we found 303 groups with 1,949 firms. The Hausman statistics is insignificant and the DW *d*-statistics and the *F*-statistics are highly significant. The Wald chi-square is also significant highly as evidence from Table 5.11.

From the results, we can observe that labour intensity is positively related to significant energy intensity of the firm. In addition, as we are trying to check the nonlinear relationship with energy intensity, the square of labour is also significant negatively. This shows an inverted U-shape relationship with energy intensity. From the estimate, we can conclude that the small and the large labour-intensive firms are energy intensive and medium labour-intensive firms are less energy intensive. Considering this, improvements of labour efficiency can be an alternative approach for energy efficiency improvement for energy-intensive pulp and paper industries in a developing country like India. In case of the capital intensity, it is negatively related with the energy intensity; this means that the higher energy-efficient firms are higher capital intensive too. Technology import intensity is also found to be negatively

Table 5.11 Result of the panel data regression (random effect)

Variables	Coefficient	Standard error	z-Statistics
Labour intensity	0.028	0.006	4.460***
Labour intensity^2	–0.006	0.010	–8.330***
Capital intensity	–0.050	0.009	–2.060***
Technology import intensity	–0.077	0.020	–3.870***
Profit margin	–0.011	–0.001	–12.350***
Size of the firm	0.004	0.003	1.470
Age of the firm	0.001	0.001	–0.210
Research and development intensity	0.598	1.557	0.380
BSE (dummy)	0.026	0.009	2.890
Labour intensity (dummy)	0.094	0.033	2.830
MNE (dummy)	0.015	0.045	0.340
Constant	0.187	0.018	10.520
Hausman chi-square(8)	15.17(0.04)	R^2 within	0.44
Wald chi-square	1,588.74***	R^2 between	0.42
DW d-statistics (9, 22) = 2.55***		R^2 overall	0.45
Number of observations	1,949	No. of groups	303

Source: Researchers' calculation based on data from CMIE
***denotes statistically significant at 1%

related to energy intensity of the firm. This indicates that firms which are importing technology either embodied or disembodied are more energy efficient. Profit intensity of the firm is found to be negatively related to the energy intensity of the firm. That implies that firms that are earning higher profits are less energy intensive. Size of the firm turned out to be positively related to energy intensity; however, it is not statistically significant as the case of research and development intensity. The listed firms are found to be more energy efficient as compared to the non-listed firms, as the result found a positive relationship between the energy intensity and BSE dummy.

As pulp and paper industries are one of the most energy-intensive industries, labour would play a major role in the level of energy efficiency and economic performance. Since labour intensity dummy has positive influence on energy intensity, higher labour-intensive industries are energy consuming. To capture effectively the role of higher labour-intensive firms on energy intensity, we have created a dummy capturing the higher labour-intensive firms. The regression result suggests a positive relation of labour intensity dummy with the energy intensity. The construction of dummy takes the value one for firms which are lower labour intensive. Therefore, the result indicates that higher labour-intensive firms are energy intensive as compared to the lower labour-intensive firms. Further, between the higher and lower labour-intensive firms (since both the constant and the labour intensity dummy are significant, we have tried to look at the difference between the higher labour industries and the lower labour-intensive industries), we can see that the higher labour-intensive firms are higher energy efficient.

5.5 Summary and Conclusion

This chapter is an attempt to understand the relationship between the labour and energy intensity for firms drawn from the pulp and paper industries in Indian manufacturing. The pulp and paper industries account for a considerable share of the industrial enterprises, production, employment and exports in the Indian economy. As per the GoI, these industries are finding itself in a competitive environment, and to facilitate its survival and growth, it is indispensable to enhance the competitiveness of the sector. In energy-intensive pulp and paper industries, improving energy efficiency by reducing energy intensity can be an important means of enhancing competitiveness, among others.

Analysis from the cross-tabulation of energy and labour intensity of the firms in this industry suggests that energy intensity is higher for the BSE-listed firms as compared to the non-listed domestic firms. However, the labour intensity is found higher for the non-listed firms as compared to the listed domestic firms. When the full sample is taken into consideration, the non-listed firms are less energy intensive as compared to the listed firms. In this case, we can also see that the non-listed firms are also lesser energy intensive as compared to the mean energy consumption of the full sample. In labour intensity, we can see that the non-listed firms are higher labour intensive as compared to the listed firms as well as from the mean of the full sample. Further, energy intensity is higher for the domestic firms and less for the foreign-owned firms. However, the energy intensity for the domestic firm and the full sample are much nearer. Looking at the labour intensity, we can observe that the labour intensity is higher for the domestic firms as compared to the foreign firms, which is even higher as compared to the full sample.

The econometric analysis of the energy intensity and other firm-specific characteristics including the labour intensity suggests that labour intensity is nonlinearly related to energy intensity. Therefore, we found substitution possibility between energy and labour in case of the pulp and paper industries in Indian manufacturing after the threshold. Hence, these industries should focus on higher employment generation. As the technology import is also found negatively related to the energy intensity of the firms, firms have to focus more on the technology import and knowledge sharing for achieving higher energy efficiency. One of the major components of the technology import is the training and know-how fees paid by the firms; hence, firms should also focus on providing training to the workforce in the firms. That in turn will help the Indian pulp and paper industries to become highly energy saving.

Acknowledgement We gratefully acknowledge comments and suggestions by Prof. B. N. Goldar and Prof. N. S. Siddharthan. The errors that remain are our own.

References

Ahluwalia IJ (1991) Productivity and growth in Indian manufacturing – trends in productivity and growth. Oxford University Press, New York/New Delhi

Allen RGD (1938) Mathematical analysis for economists. St. Martin's Press, New York

Balasubrahmanya MH (2006) Labour productivity, energy intensity and economic performance in small enterprises: a study of brick enterprises cluster in India. Energy Conver Manage 47:763–777

Barnett AH, Reutter K, Thompson H (1998) Electricity substitution: some local industrial evidence. Energy Econ 20:411–419

Caloghiro Y, Mourelatos A, Thompson H (1997) Industrial energy substitution during the 1980s in the Greek economy. Energy Econ 19:476–491

Cameron T, Schwartz SL (1980) Inflationary expectations and the demand for capital, labor, and energy in Canadian manufacturing industries. In: Ziemba WT et al (eds) Energy policy modeling: U.S. and Canadian experiences. Matinus Nijhoff Publishing, Boston

Chang K (1994) Capital-energy substitution and the multi-level CES production function. Energy Econ 16:22–26

Chaudhuri S (2002) Economic reforms and industrial structure in India. Econ Pol Wkly 37(02):155–162

Christensen LR, Jorgenson D, Lau LJ (1971) Conjugate duality and the transcendental logarithmic production function. Econometrica 39:255–256

Cohen M (1998) Monitoring and enforcement of environmental policy. In: Tietenberg T, Folmer H (eds) International yearbook of environmental and resource economics, vol III. Edward Elgar Publishers, Northampton

Das D, Wadhwa D, Kalita G (2009) The employment potential of labor intensive industries in India's organized manufacturing. Working paper no. 236. Indian Council for Research on International Economic Relations, New Delhi

Denison EF (1974) Accounting for United States economic growth 1929 to 1969. Brookings Institution, Washington, DC

Denison EF (1979) Accounting for slower economic growth. Brookings Institution, Washington, DC

Denison EF (1985) Trends in American economic growth 1929–1982. Brookings Institution, Washington, DC

Denny M, Fuss M, Waverman L (1981) Substitution possibilities for energy: evidence from US and Canadian manufacturing industries. In: Berndt ER, Field BC (eds) Modeling and measuring natural resource substitution. MIT Press, Cambridge

Doonan J, Lanoie P, Laplante B (2005) Determinants of environment performance in Canadian pulp and paper industries: an assessment from inside the industry. Ecol Econ 55:73–84

Easterly W, Levine R (2002) Chapter 3: It's not factor accumulation: stylized facts and growth models. In: Klaus S-H (ed) Economic growth: sources, trends, and cycles, vol 6, 1st edn. Central Bank of Chile, Santiago, pp 061–114

Felipe J (1997) Total factor productivity growth in East Asia: a critical survey, EDRC report series number 65, Economics and Development Resource Center, Asian Development Bank

Foulon J, Lanoie P, Laplante B (2002) Incentives for pollution control: regulation or information? J Environ Econ Manage 44:169–187

Ganguli I, Roy J (1995) Oil demand elasticities in India. Indian J Appl Econ 5(1):75–87

Goldar B (2000) Employment growth in organized manufacturing in India. Econ Pol Wkly 35(14):1191–1195

Goldar B (2010) Energy intensity of Indian manufacturing firms: effect of energy prices, technology and other firm characteristics. Paper presented during the conference on frontier issues in technology, Development and Environment at MSE, Chennai

Hogan W, Jorgenson D (1991) Productivity trends and the cost of reducing CO_2 emissions. Energy J 12(1):67–85

Hseu JS, Shang JK (2005) Productivity changes of pulp and paper industry in OECD countries 1991–2000: a non-parametric malmquist approach. For Policy Econ 7:411–422

Hudson EA, Jorgenson D (1974) US energy policy and economic growth 1975–2000. Bell J Econ Manage Sci 5:461–514

Jha R, Murty MN, Paul S, Rao BB (1993) An analysis of technological change, factor substitution and economies of scale in manufacturing industries in India. Appl Econ 25:1337–1343

Jorgenson DW, Fraumeni BM (1981) Relative prices and technical change. In: Berndt ER, Fields B (eds) Modeling and measuring natural resources substitution. MIT Press, Cambridge

Jorgenson DW, Gollop FM, Fraumeni M (1987) Productivity and U.S. economic growth. North Holland, Amsterdam/Oxford

Kumar A (2003) Energy intensity: a quantitative exploration for Indian manufacturing. IGIDR Working paper no. 152. http://dx.doi.org/10.2139/ssrn.468440

Lashof D, Tirpak D (eds) (1990) Policy options for stabilizing global climate: report to Congress, Executive summary, US Environmental Protection Agency, No. 21

Li X, Buongiorno J, Ince PJ (2004) Effects of size and age on the survival and growth of pulp and paper mills. J For Econ 10:3–9

Ma H, Oxley L, Gibson J (2009) Substitution possibilities and determinants of energy intensity for China. Energy Policy 37:1793–1804

Mahmud S (2000) The energy demand in the manufacturing sector of Pakistan: some further results. Energy Econ 22:641–648

Mongia P, Sathaye J (1998a) Productivity trends in India's energy intensive industries: a growth accounting analysis, Lawrence Berkeley National Laboratory. Working paper no. 41838, Berkeley, CA

Mongia P, Sathaye J (1998b) Productivity growth and technical change in India's energy intensive industries – a survey, Lawrence Berkeley National Laboratory. Working paper no. 41840, Berkeley, CA

Mongia P, Schumacher K, Sathaye J (2001) Policy reforms and productivity growth in India's energy intensive industries. Energy Policy 29:715–724

Nagaraj R (2004) Fall in organized manufacturing employment – a brief note. Econ Pol Wkly 39(30):3387–3390

Pradhan G, Barik K (1999) Total factor productivity growth in developing economies: a study of selected industries in India. Econ Pol Wkly 34(31):M92–M97

Roy J (1992) Demand for energy in Indian manufacturing industries. Daya Publishing, New Delhi

Roy J, Sathaye J, Sanstad A, Mongia P, Schumacher K (1999) Productivity trends in India's energy intensive industries. Energy J 20(3):33–61

Sahu SK, Narayanan K (2010) Determinants of energy intensity in Indian manufacturing industries: a firm level analysis. MPRA paper no. 21646, University Library of Munich, Munich

Sahu SK, Narayanan K (2011) Determinants of energy intensity in Indian manufacturing industries: a firm level study. Eurasian J Econ Bus 4(8):13–30

Sarkar S, Roy J (1995) Inter-fuel substitution during post oil embargo period - case study of two energy intensive manufacturing industries in India. The Indian Econ J 43(2):33–46

Sathaye JA, Ravindranath NH (1998) Climate change mitigation in the energy and forestry sectors of developing countries. Annu Rev Eng Environ 23:387–437

Schumacher K, Sathaye J (1999) India's pulp and paper industry: productivity and energy efficiency. Ernest Orlando Lawrence Berkeley National Laboratory, LBNL-41843

Solow RM (1957) Technical change and the aggregate production function. Rev Econ Stat 39:312–320

Takayama A (1993) Analytical methods in economics. University of Michigan Press, Ann Harbor

Uma R, Unni J (2004) Unorganized and organized manufacturing in India: potential for employment generating growth. Econ Pol Wkly 39(41):4568–4580

UNFCCC (1998) Kyoto protocol to the United Nations Framework Convention on climate change, available at http://unfccc.int/resource/docs/convkp/kpeng.pdf

Varian HR (1984) Microeconomic analysis. W. W. Norton & Company, New York

Weyant J, Davidson O, Dowlatabadi H, Edmonds J, Grubb M, Parson EA, Richels R, Rotmans J, Shukla PR, Tol RSJ, Cline W, Fankhauser S (1996) Integrated assessment of climate change: an overview and comparison of approaches and results. In: Bruce JP, Lee H, Erik HF (eds) Climate change 1995 – economic and social dimensions of climate change. Cambridge University Press, New York

World Bank (2000) Greening industry: new roles for communities, markets, and governments. World Bank/Oxford University Press, Washington, DC

Yi F (2000) Dynamic energy-demand models: a comparison. Energy Econ 22:285–297

Chapter 6
Impact of Remittances on Poverty in India: Empirical Evidence

Rashmi Banga and Pritish Kumar Sahu

6.1 Introduction

Remittances have been an important source of external funding for India. The span of Indian diaspora stretches across the globe in all continents. The Ministry of Overseas Indian Affairs has registered the presence of non-resident Indians (NRIs) in 180 of the 183 countries of the world. The numbers have varied from just two in Lebanon to almost a million in the USA. Estimated at over 30 million, India ranks second to Chinese diaspora. The growing number of migrants from India has added to the remittance inflow over the years. Data in this regard reveals that, even though the remittance flows to the Indian economy during the 1980s remained more or less stable, the postreform period from 1991 onwards has experienced a significant increase in remittances. There has been an annual average trend growth of 16% during the period 1990 to 2008. In 2008, after the outbreak of economic crisis, India reported 34% growth over 2007.[1]

The surging inflow of remittances to the Indian economy has received much attention worldwide as it has emerged as single largest recipient with more than one-tenth share in global remittances.[2] Even during the current economic slowdown,

---

[1] However, according to RBI, there has been a 13% decline in remittances at $22.8 billion during the first half (January–June) of the calendar year 2009, against $26.2 billion in the same period last year.

[2] However, the share of international remittance inflow to India as proportion of developing country's inflow stood nearly 16% in the year 2008.

R. Banga (✉)
Unit of Economic Cooperation and Integration Among
Developing Countries, UNCTAD, Geneva
e-mail: rashmibanga@yahoo.com

P.K. Sahu
Faculty of Business and Law, Multimedia University, Melaka, Malaysia
e-mail: epritishkumar9@gmail.com

N.S. Siddharthan and K. Narayanan (eds.), *Human Capital and Development: The Indian Experience*, DOI 10.1007/978-81-322-0857-0_6, © Springer India 2013

a recent World Bank Report[3] reveals that India continues to be one of the highest global remittance-receiving country for the year 2010 ($53 billion), whereas the remittance flows to the many developing countries declined. Given that around one-third of the world's poor[4] reside in India, India makes an interesting case study for the analysis of impact of remittances on poverty.

Though there is a growing literature on the impact of remittances on development, very few studies have empirically estimated the impact of remittances on development in general, and on poverty in particular, in the developing countries. This chapter estimates the impact of remittances on poverty in India using the methodology applied by other studies (IMF 2005). It also undertakes a time-series analysis at a more micro-level for estimating impact of remittances on poverty in Kerala, which is one of the top remittance-receiving states in India. Granger causality tests are undertaken with respect to remittance flow and different indicators of poverty in India. This test is conducted for the period 1973–1974 to 2008–2009 to have insights into the channels through which the impact of remittances is transmitted to reduction in poverty. Similar analyses are undertaken for the highest remittance-receiving state of India, namely, Kerala.

The rest of the chapter is organised as follows: Sect. 6.2 provides a review of literature on migration and development, including the studies on remittances and poverty; Sect. 6.3 highlights the trends in remittances in India in particular; Sect. 6.4 presents the model and the results estimating the impact of remittances on poverty in India; Sect. 6.5 reports the results with respect to Kerala; Sect. 6.6 concludes with policy implications.

6.2 Remittances and Economic Development: Review of Literature

The official recorded remittances are much lower than the actual remittances that take place through official and unofficial channels. Remittances through informal channels could add at least 50% to the globally recorded flows (World Bank 2006, *ibidem*, p. 85). Despite this under-reporting, many studies have highlighted the important nexus between the international migration, remittances and development. This section summarises the existing studies, which examine this nexus, especially in the context of developing countries.

Several studies have pointed out that the more the inflow of remittances, the healthier the recipient country will be. In times of economic distress, remittances

[3] Remittance flows to developing countries is expected to be $317 billion in 2009, down from an estimated $328 billion in 2008 (Migration and Development brief, World Bank, 3 November 2009).

[4] According to 2005 World Bank estimates, about 456 million Indians (42% of the total Indian population) now live under the global poverty line of $1.25 per day (PPP). This means that a third of the global poor now reside in India.

may actually be countercyclical to the extent that migrants are motivated by altruism and send more money home. The stability of these inflows also opens up an opportunity for developing countries to borrow at lower cost in international capital markets by securitizing future flows of remittances (IMF 2005). As remittance receipts are widely dispersed, they may not cause the real exchange rate to appreciate.

Pant (2008) argues that whether remittances are utilised for consumption or purchasing houses, or other investments, they produce positive impact on the economy by stimulating demand for other goods and services. Migrants provide different forms of capital that have developmental impact on their countries of origin. These impacts may be in the form of financial, social, cultural, political and/or economic impacts. The impact can be examined at both micro-level, like in case of households, and macro-level like impact on GDP growth, poverty and development.

6.2.1 Link Between Remittances and Household Development

Majority of the existing studies, which focus on the impact of migration on household members left behind, have shown positive impact in both short run and long run. Rapoport and Docquier (2006) show how the household members who are left behind use migrants' remittances. Remittances are used to repay loans taken to finance migration or education and insurance and strategic motives. It also directly contributes to household income, allowing households to purchase more assets; enables higher investment in business; and facilitates buying more goods, including education and health inputs. Yang (2004) and Woodruff and Zenteno (2001) suggest that at the household level, remittances can spur entrepreneurial activity. Hildebrandt and McKenzie (2005) emphasise the knowledge transfer and change in attitudes of the remaining family members of the migrants. For example, they find that the knowledge about contraceptives increased with emigration of household members from Mexico to the USA.

6.2.2 Link Between Remittances and GDP

Studies examining the relationship between remittances and GDP growth show mixed result. Faini (2002, 2003) finds a positive relationship between growth and remittances using cross-country data. Similarly, positive relationship between the two is also supported by several studies for Mexican economy. For example, Adelman and Taylor (1990) find that 'every dollar Mexican migrants send back home or bring back with them increases Mexico's GNP from anywhere between US$ 2.69 and US$ 3.17, depending on which household income group received the remittances'. Durand et al. (1996) suggest that for every US$2 billion in remittances that entered Mexico, production in the economy increased by over US$6.5

billion dollars. Ekanayake and Halkides (2008) examine the impact of foreign remittances and foreign direct investment on the economic growth of developing countries. The study uses annual data of a large group of developing countries covering Asia, Africa and Latin America and the Caribbean for the period 1980–2006. They find that both remittances and foreign direct investment significantly promote growth in developing countries. However, this positive relationship is challenged in several studies, e.g. Spatafora (2005) finds that there is no direct link between real per capita output growth and remittances. Chami et al. (2005), using panel data for 113 developing countries, find that remittances have a negative effect on economic growth.

6.2.3 *Link Between Remittance, Consumption and Investment*

Many studies examine the relationship between remittances and investments in the home countries. Barjas et al. (2009) point out that for developing countries, remittances are large relative to other financial flows.[5] They find that in the last 10-year period, remittance flows have become as large as foreign direct investment (FDI) flows to developing countries, amounting on an average of about one-third of export earnings, more than twice the private capital flows, almost 10 times official capital flows and more than 12 times official transfers. In light of this, developing countries should capitalise this huge amount of remittance inflows and use it for investment to promote development and the growth. Empirical evidence in this regard shows that the inflow of remittances by the migrant workers and professionals from an underdeveloped and developing country helps in increasing the investment activities in the recipient country. Asiedu (2003) reveals that nearly 30% of remittances are used for the purpose of investment and construction of house in Ghana. Similarly, according to Drinkwater et al. (2003), if the primary income earner remains at home and continues to maintain the household, earnings from migration are more easily diverted to savings and investment. By using 1988 survey of 1,526 Egyptian migrants, McCormick and Wahba (2001) attempt to find the probability of a migrant becoming an entrepreneur/employer/self-employed person or a business owner—upon his/her return from working abroad. Even though the results are different for literate and illiterate migrants, the general conclusion derived was that two factors, namely, time spent working abroad and total amount of money saved abroad, have positive and significant effect on the likelihood of migrants becoming entrepreneurs on their return to the home country.

Adams (2005a) examines the impact of remittances on the spending behaviour of household for consumption and investments, in both the rural and urban Guatemala. The study takes the data from the 2000 survey of 7,276 households and compares

[5] In 2004 official international remittances were estimated at $93 billion per year (Ratha 2003), making them about twice as large as the level of official aid-related flows to developing countries.

the marginal budget share of remittance-receiving and non-remittance-receiving household on six consumption and investment goods. The findings show that the households receiving international remittances spend more at the margin on investment goods, especially, on housing and education, and spend less, at the margin, on food items. Similarly, Yang (2004) analyses how the exchange rate shocks during 1997 due to the Asian financial crisis affected the expenditure pattern of 1,646 Philippine households receiving international remittances. Of the several findings in this chapter, one of its findings shows that favourable exchange rate shocks (i.e. more remittance income as a result of favourable exchange rate shocks) increase the investment of remittance-receiving household in entrepreneurial activities specifically in transportation, communication and manufacturing enterprises.

6.2.4 Link Between Remittances, Poverty and Welfare

The flow of remittances remains more or less stable irrespective of the economic condition of the recipient country.[6] Remittances are expected to reduce poverty as they may be directly received by the poor. The impact of remittances on reduction of poverty can be understood from both micro- and macro-perspectives. However, to capture this impact, there is no formal framework (Chimhowu et al. 2005). But it is evident and reasonable to assume that the amount of transfer done by the migrants to the family members back home does have some overall impact in reducing the poverty. Uruci and Gedeshi (2003) using survey of long-term legal immigrants find that majority of the international migrants (69.7%) send their money in order to meet 'the essential needs of the family'.

Very few studies explicitly address the link between remittances and poverty. Adams and Page (2005) used household surveys of 71 developing countries to examine the impact of international migration on poverty. Controlling for the level of income, income inequality and geographical region, they find that international remittances have a strong statistically significant negative impact on poverty. A 10% increase in the share of remittances in a country's GDP led to a reduction of 1.6% of people living in poverty. Campos and de Palomo (2002) find that in 2000, the remittances helped reduce the national poverty rate by 4.2% in El Salvador as well as reduced the Gini coefficient from 0.55 to 0.53.

Adams (2004) finds that the squared poverty gap measure in Guatemala declined by 19.8% when international remittances were included as a part of the total household income. López-Cordova (2005) finds that remittances have a statistically significant impact in reducing poverty in Mexico at the municipal level. Gustafsson and Makonnen (1993) used the data of 7,680 households from 1986 to 1987 survey to examine the impact of remittances on poverty and welfare in rural and urban

---

[6] In the wake of the Asian financial crisis in the late 1990s, remittances to developing countries continued to rise even though FDI and official aid flows declined (World Bank 2004).

Lesotho. They found that 35% of household incomes come from the remittances. It shows that if the remittances were set to zero, the average per capita household consumption would fall by 32% and the poverty head count index would increase by 26%. In addition, a cessation of remittances would lead to a 52% increase in the poverty gap index. A similar study by Taylor et al. (2005) used the data of 1,782 household from the 2003 survey of rural Mexico to show the impact of international remittances on poverty. The study estimates that poverty headcount and poverty gap indices would decline by 0.77 and 0.53, respectively, with 10% increase in international remittances.

6.2.5 Link Between Remittances and Foreign Exchange

Remittances constitute one of the major and more resilient sources of foreign exchange earnings for many developing countries. Remittances ease the short-run foreign exchange constraints at times when the foreign investment and the other official assistance decline due to external factors. Bouhga-Hagbe (2004) explain the importance of remittances to Morocco as a source of foreign exchange that could be used positively for development. Similarly, Rajan and Subramanyam (2005) also find that remittances have more positive impact on the exchange rate than aid.

6.2.6 Link Between Remittances and Employment

Very few studies have estimated the macroeconomic impact of remittances on the employment of the recipient country. At micro-level, studies suggest mixed results. Frank (2001) argues that the families receiving international remittances severely curtail their work efforts. Similarly, Rodriguez and Tiongson (2001) for Funkhouser E (1992) for Managua conclude that remittances reduce employment. However, they do not take into account of endogeneity of remittances with respect to labour supply. Rodriguez and Tiongson (2001) conclude that when migration occurs, non-migrant relatives receive remittances, which they perceive as additional non-labour income. An increase in non-labour income then reduces their participation in local labour markets. In contrast to these studies, Cox-Edwards and Rodriguez-Oreggia (2009) find that remittances have no impact on the labour supply of household members in Mexico. However, at macro-level, when the inflow of remittances is used for the investment, the non-migrated families get benefited by seeking employment.

Overall, literature provides sufficient evidence to support the hypothesis that remittances are beneficial to the recipient countries and can significantly affect poverty and development. However, most of the studies are survey-based, and very few empirical studies exist which are able to quantify the impact of remittances on poverty levels in the developing countries.

6.3 Trends in Migration and Remittances

6.3.1 Trends in Global Remittances

Officially recorded remittance flows to developing countries proved to be more resilient to the crisis and recovered quickly to reach $325 billion in 2010. They therefore emerged as an important source of external funding for developing countries. At the country level, India, China and Mexico received around 59% of total remittances, despite the weak job market in many developed countries. Table 6.1 shows top ten remittance-recipient countries.

6.3.2 Trends in Indian Migration and Remittances

The pace of migration from India accelerated in the post economic reforms of 1991. Accordingly, there has been a rapid increase in remittances since the early 1990s. The measurement of Indian migrants to the rest of the world is not straightforward as it is difficult to count all single movement of people from the region. However, the recent data reveals that the Indian diaspora spreads across the globe. Table 6.2 summarises the approximate number of overseas Indians.

It is noteworthy to mention that the new migration of labour have taken a reverse turn globally due to the onset of global economic crisis. However, the Indian migration to other countries has experienced no sign of decline in the recent past. However, the rate of growth of migration has declined but in absolute term, there has been a substantial increase over the past years. The official data in this regard reveals that nearly 0.85 million population have been granted immigration clearance during the

Table 6.1 Top 10 recipients of remittances during the year 2009

Top 10 countries	US $ billion	Top 10 countries	%age of GDP
India	55	Tajikistan	35
China	51	Tonga	28
Mexico	23	Lesotho	25
Philippines	21	Kyrgyz Rep	28
France	16	Moldova	23
Germany	12	Nepal	22
Bangladesh	11	Samoa	22
Belgium	10	Lebanon	22
Spain	10	Honduras	19
Nigeria	10	Guyana	17

Source: Development Prospects Group, World Bank (2011)

Table 6.2 Estimated size of overseas Indian community: top 15 countries (December 2001)

Country	PIOs	Indian citizen	Stateless	Total population
Myanmar	2,500,000	2,000	400,000	2,902,000
USA	NA	NA	NA	1,678,765
Malaysia	1,600,000	15,000	50,000	1,665,000
Saudi Arabia	–	1,500,000	–	1,500,000
UK	NA	NA	NA	1,200,000
South Africa	NA	NA	NA	1,000,000
UAE	50,000	900,000	–	950,000
Canada	700,000	150,000	1,000	851,000
Mauritius	704,640	11,116	–	715,756
Trinidad and Tobago	500,000	600	–	500,600
Guyana	395,250	100	–	395,350
Fiji	336,579	250	–	336,829
Oman	1,000	311,000	–	312,000
Singapore	217,000	9,000	81,000	307,000
Kuwait	1,000	294,000	–	295,000

Source: Compiled from the Report of High Level Committee on Indian Diaspora
Note: *PIOs* – Persons of Indian Origin

year 2008 against 0.8 million during 2007. Table 6.3 shows the immigration clearance to top destination countries in recent years.

At a more disaggregated level, the official data on the state-wise emigration clearance shows that Kerala is the state with highest immigration clearance in India in 2008 (Table 6.4). The share of Uttar Pradesh[7] has increased drastically in recent years and has become second only to Kerala during the year 2008 and up to March 2009. On the other hand, the share of major states such as Tamil Nadu, Andhra Pradesh and Maharashtra in the total immigration clearance has experienced a declining trend in recent years.

The increasing number of migration from India has led to an increase in the remittance inflow into the country. Over the years, India has experienced a substantial increase in the remittance inflow. As per the RBI recognition, the inflow of remittances to India is of two types, namely, direct inward remittance and local withdrawal from the NRI accounts. The inward remittances are direct transfer of funds from a person abroad to a person in India. Such transfers are generally meant for providing family support. However, the NRI deposit accounts[8] are created with the aim to attract the foreign capital and foreign currency to boost the economy. RBI recognises the foreign currency NRI deposits as debt[9] and withdrawal from

[7] It is also the most populous state in India with an estimated 190 million people (around 17% of India's population) as of July 2008.

[8] This scheme has been authorised by the GOI in 1970, and it gives the choice to the depositors for holding deposits either in terms of Indian currency or in terms of foreign currency.

[9] This is because the principal amount can be withdrawn by the NRI depositors with interest when they wish.

Table 6.3 Distribution of annual labour outflows from India to major destination

Countries	2002	2004	2006	2007	2008	Up to March 2009
UAE	95,034	175,262	254,774	312,695	349,827	35,905
Saudi Arabia	99,453	12,322	134,059	195,437	228,406	80,962
Malaysia	10,512	31,464	36,500	30,916	21,123	4,611
Qatar	12,596	16,325	76,324	88,483	82,937	11,953
Oman	41,209	33,275	67,992	95,462	89,659	17,175
Kuwait	4,859	52,064	47,449	48,467	35,562	10,982
Bahrain	20,807	22,980	37,688	29,967	31,924	6,806
Maldives	–	3,233	4,671	ECNR	ECNR	ECNR
Mauritius	–	3,544	1,795	ECNR	ECNR	ECNR
Jordan	–	2,576	1,485	1,254	1,377	242
Other	83,193	121,915	14,175	6,772	7,786	2,011
Total	367,663	474,960	676,912	809,453	848,601	170,647

Source: Compiled from Annual Report (2008–2009), Ministry of Overseas Indian Affairs
ECNR Emigration Clearance not Reported

Table 6.4 Immigration clearance of workers granted during 2002–2008: state-wise shares

Ranks (in 2008)	States	2002	2004	2006	2007	2008	Up to 31st March 2009
1	Kerala	22.29	13.37	17.74	18.59	21.29	20.58
2	UP	5.25	5.77	9.77	11.32	16.41	20.48
3	Tamil Nadu	21.53	22.94	22.99	18.64	15.18	13.33
4	Andhra Pradesh	10.45	15.28	14.43	12.98	11.49	11.12
5	Rajasthan	6.32	7.39	7.42	8.76	7.61	6.63
6	Bihar	5.23	4.59	5.39	6.40	7.15	7.66
7	Punjab	5.34	5.33	5.81	6.66	6.42	4.38
8	West Bengal	2.27	1.89	2.21	3.07	3.07	3.25
9	Maharashtra	6.93	6.04	2.27	2.66	2.92	3.20
10	Karnataka	3.82	4.05	3.60	3.34	2.64	3.22
11	Gujarat	3.24	4.68	1.96	2.48	1.85	1.69
12	Orissa	0.47	1.47	0.61	0.83	1.05	1.05
13	Delhi	1.09	1.27	1.34	0.66	0.53	0.41
14	Madhya Pradesh	2.02	1.87	1.04	0.45	0.27	0.31
15	Haryana	0.12	0.27	0.03	0.23	0.21	0.20
	Others	3.63	3.78	2.79	2.58	1.63	2.23
	Total	100	100	100	100	100	100

Source: Offices of the Protectors of Emigrants
Note: The states have been ranked in descending order with 2008 migration data

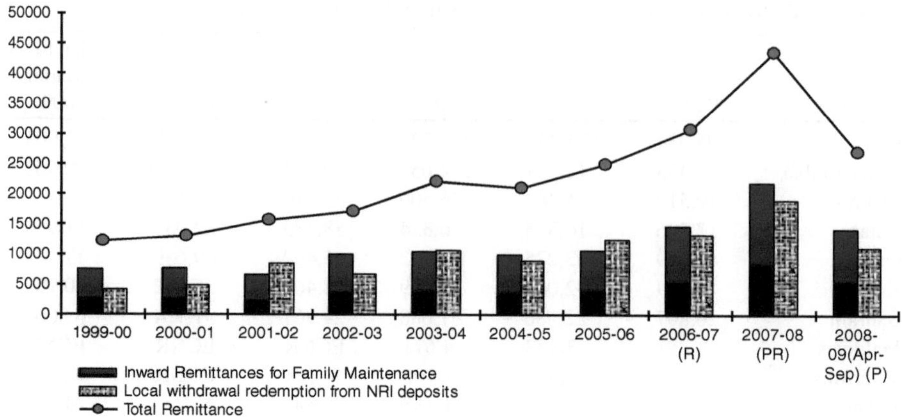

Fig. 6.1 Trends and composition of remittances transfer (Source: Invisibles in India's balance of payments, 'RBI Bulletin', March 2009) Notes: *R* revised, *PR* partially revised, *P* preliminary

rupee-denominated deposits as remittances. To understand this, Fig. 6.1 shows in detail the remittance flow and its composition over the period.

It is evident that the remittance transfer to India has shown an increasing trend over the year irrespective of the global financial crisis (Table 6.5). This may be attributed to a number of factors, such as depreciation of rupee resulting in the rise in inflows through rupee-denominated NRI accounts to take advantage of the depreciation, hike in interest rate ceilings on NRI deposits since September 2008, and uncertainties in oil prices, which might have induced the workers to remit their money to India as a hedging mechanism due to its relatively better growth prospects.[10]

The peculiar picture which we capture in the trends and composition of remittances transfer shows that the local withdrawals to the total remittances transfer which accounted about 50% in the first half of the 1990s declined to 29% in the latter half (Table 6.6). However, since 2003–2004 there has been relatively rising significance of the local withdrawal route in the total remittances transfer. The estimated local withdrawals in the total remittances during the year 2007–2008 increased to 43.5% against the 42.8% during the same period last year.

Remittances have steadily grown as a percentage of GDP. It increased from less than 1% in 1990 to 2.8% in 2000 and further to 6.2% in 2008 (Fig. 6.2).

This indicates that remittances may have had an impact in removing people out of poverty over time in India. Given the limited comparable data on poverty indicators for India,[11] the poverty ratio with respect to national poverty line is used. The existing trends on poverty indicators reveal that there has been a fall in poverty ratio in India from 54.9% in 1973–1974 to 19.3% in 2006–2007 (Table 6.7). To capture the extent of inequality, Lorenz ratio is used, as reported by Ministry of Rural Development, Government of India (10895) (INDIASTAT). Lorenz ratio is estimated from NSS consumption expenditure distribution of the respective years.

---

[10] RBI, Monthly Bulletin, April 2010.

[11] World Development Indicators, World Bank have very few observations for India.

Table 6.5 India's workers' remittances, compensation of employees and migrant transfers, credit (US $ million)

Year	Inflow	Outflow	Outflow as % age of inflow
1980	2,757	29	1.05
1981	2,301	15	0.65
1982	2,618	14	0.53
1983	2,660	40	1.50
1984	2,295	27	1.18
1985	2,469	31	1.26
1986	2,240	42	1.88
1987	2,665	65	2.44
1988	2,315	93	4.02
1989	2,614	99	3.79
1990	2,384	106	4.45
1991	3,289	52	1.58
1992	2,897	68	2.35
1993	3,523	259	7.35
1994	5,857	351	5.99
1995	6,223	419	6.73
1996	8,766	538	6.14
1997	10,331	162	1.57
1998	9,479	44	0.46
1999	11,124	36	0.32
2000	12,890	486	3.77
2001	14,273	751	5.26
2002	15,736	1,187	7.54
2003	20,999	1,265	6.02
2004	18,750	1,653	8.81
2005	22,125	1,341	6.06
2006	28,334	1,580	5.58
2007	37,217	1,580	4.25
2008	51,581	1,580	3.06
2009e	47,000	–	

Source: World Bank, Migration and Development Brief 11 (November 2009)

6.4 Impact of Remittances on Poverty: Methodology and Results

6.4.1 Methodology

Very limited empirical literature exists on macroeconomic impact of remittance on poverty. However, recent cross-country studies are increasingly finding evidence of positive impact of remittances on reducing poverty. World Bank study by Adams and Page (2005) shows that a 10% increase in per capita official international

Table 6.6 Inflows and outflows from NRI deposits, local withdrawals and remittances

Year	Inflows	Outflows	Local withdrawals from NRI deposits	Private transfers (included in current account of BoP)	Local withdrawals as % age of private transfers
1999–2000	7,405	5,865	4,120	12,290	33.5
2000–2001	8,988	6,672	4,727	13,065	36.2
2001–2002	11,435	8,681	8,546	15,760	54.2
2002–2003	10,214	7,236	6,644	17,189	38.6
2003–2004	14,281	10,639	10,585	22,182	47.7
2004–2005	8,071	9,035	8,907	21,075	42.3
2005–2006	17,835	15,046	12,454	24,951	49.9
2006–2007 (R)	19,914	15,593	13,208	30,835	42.8
2007–2008 (PR)	29,401	29,222	18,919	43,506	43.5
2008–2009 (April–September) (P)	18,237	17,164	11,217	27,042	41.5
2007–2008 (April–September) (PR)	12,227	12,305	7,891	18,025	43.8

Source: Invisibles in India's Balance of Payments: An Analysis of Trade in Services, Remittances and Income, RBI, 16 March 2009
Notes: *P* provisional, *PR* partially revised, *R* revised

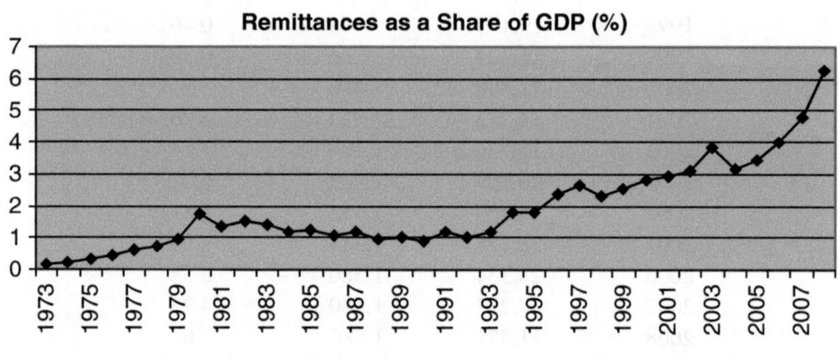

Fig. 6.2 Remittances as a share of GDP in India: 1973–2008 (Source: Remittance data is taken from World Bank, Migration Development Brief and GDP data from RBI)

remittances will lead, on average, to a 3.5% decline in the share of people living in poverty. Similarly, IMF (2007) study finds that on average, a 10% increase in the share of remittances in a country's GDP is associated with about a 1.5% fall in headcount poverty and 1.1% fall in poverty gap.

Following Ravallion (1997) and Ravallion and Chen (1997), poverty is taken as a function of per capita income, some measure of income distribution and the remittances to GDP ratio.[12] The baseline specification is

[12] Similar model is estimated by IMF 2005.

Table 6.7 Poverty ratio in India: 1973–1974 to 2006–2007

Indices of poverty and inequality in terms of poverty ratio and Lorenz ratio in India (1973–1974, 1977–1978, 1983–1984, 1987–1988,1993–1994 and 2004–2005)			
	Poverty ratio	Lorenz ratio	
Year	Total	Rural	Urban
1973–1974	54.9	0.27	0.301
1977–1978	51.3	0.33	0.345
1983–1984	44.5	0.29	0.33
1987–1988	38.9	0.29	0.354
1993–1994	36	0.28	0.339
1999–2000	26.1		
2004–2005		0.3	0.376
2006–2007	19.3		

Source: Ministry of Rural Development, Government of India (10895), INDIASTAT

$$\log\left(\mathrm{POV}_{it}\right)=\alpha_1+\alpha_2\log\left(\mathrm{PCY}_{it}\right)+\alpha_3\log\left(\mathrm{INEQ}_{it}\right)+\alpha_4\log\left(\mathrm{REM}_{it}\right)+\varepsilon_{it} \quad (6.1)$$
$$\left(\text{where } i=1\ldots N,\quad t-1\ldots T_i\right),$$

where POV_{it} is poverty ratio in India at time t, α_1 is the intercept, PCY is per capita income, INEQ is income inequality as measured by the Lorenz ratio, and REM is remittances to GDP ratio. Given low number of observations, three-stage least squares may not be right to estimate.

The model expects that poverty is reduced as per capita income rises; hence, α_2 is expected to be negative. Based on previous studies, we expect higher poverty to be associated with greater income inequality; hence, α_3 is expected to be positive. Controlling for these two variables, the model estimates the sign and magnitude of α_4, which indicates the direct impact of share of remittances in GDP on poverty.

To measure poverty, three indicators are used: poverty headcount ratio at $1.25 a day (PPP) (%age of population), poverty gap at $1.25 a day (PPP) (%) and poverty gap at $2 a day (PPP) (%). Poverty gap measures the mean distance below the poverty line as a proportion of the poverty line and captures how poor the poor are, i.e. how far below the poverty line the average poor person's income is. Gini coefficient is used as a measure of inequality. Remittances are expressed as a ratio of the GDP of recipient countries. Per capita income variable used is per capita GDP in constant US$2,000. The log transformation of all the variables allows us to interpret the coefficients as elasticities.

Impact of remittances as a share of GDP on poverty indicators is undertaken by estimating Eq. 6.1 for the period 1973–1974 to 2006–2007.

With respect to India, estimates of poverty and inequality indicators are available only after a gap of some years (Table 6.7). However, to estimate the impact of share of remittances in GDP on poverty, we assume that the decline in poverty and inequality levels is equally distributed between the gap years.

Table 6.8 Time-series estimates: dependent variables, remittances as a share of GDP in India (1973–2005)

Independent variables	Dependent variable – poverty headcount ratio at $1.25 a day (PPP) (% age of population)
Remittances as a share of GDP	–0.17***
	(–6.52)
Lorenz ratio	1.20***
	(7.76)
Per capita income (PCY)	–0.23**
	(–2.23)
Constant	6.95***
	(16.43)
Observations	32
Chi-square	1615.87

Source: Authors' estimates. Data is taken from World Development Indicators
Note: ***indicates significance at 1% level

Given the paucity of data, another methodology is also applied to substantiate the regression estimates. Time-series analysis is undertaken to examine the causality of relationship between remittances and poverty.

6.4.2 Empirical Res ults

The results of estimations are reported in Table 6.8. The results show that in India, remittances have a negative impact on poverty ratio, as defined by national poverty line. A 10% increase in remittances as a share of GDP will lead to a fall of 1.7% in poverty ratio. This is much lower than the impact estimated for the developing countries and for the Asian developing countries. As expected, inequality is found to be positively associated with poverty ratio, while higher per capita income reduces poverty ratio. However, these results should be taken only as indicative due to the paucity of data on poverty ratio and the assumption adopted thereby.

Given the limitations of the above methodology, we undertake Granger causality tests between remittances and some indicators of poverty, e.g. private consumption expenditure, gross fixed capital formation (GFCF) and personal disposable income. In order to do this, we need to perform the standard stationarity tests. The prime purpose of these tests is to avoid any spurious result. The results of stationarity tests are reported in Appendix 1.

For the period 1970–1971 to 2007–2008, the Granger causality test (1969) is used to find out if the change in remittances causes change in poverty-related indicators like per capita income, private consumption expenditure, gross fixed capital formation (GFCG) and personal disposable income. Given the lag with

Table 6.9 Pairwise Granger causality between the remittances and other macro-variables

Direction of causality/null hypothesis	Number of lags	Observations (no. of years)	*F*-Value	Significance	Decision
Remittances do not Granger cause PCY	2	34	3.379	Sign at 5%	Reject
PCY does not Granger cause remittances	2	34	3.413	Sign at 5%	Reject
Remittance does not Granger cause pvt. consumption expenditure	2	34	3.379	Sign at 5%	Reject
Pvt. consumption expenditure does not Granger cause remittances	2	34	3.413	Sign at 5%	Reject
GFCF does not Granger cause remittances	4	31	1.40	Not sign	Do not reject
Remittance does not Granger cause GFCF	4	31	2.267	Sign at 10%	Reject
Disposable income does not Granger cause remittances	2	34	4.674	Sign at 5%	Reject
Remittance does not Granger cause pvt. final consumption exp.	2	34	4.052	Sign at 5%	Reject

Source: Authors' estimates

which poverty estimates are made available for India, a direct Granger causality test between remittances and poverty ratio is not undertaken.

The main idea of causality is quite simple, if A causes B, then changes in A should precede changes in B (Pindyck and Rubinfeld 1998). To show this, the Granger causality test critically depends on the number of lagged terms introduced in the model. The results of the test are presented in Table 6.9. In each case, the null hypothesis is that the remittances do not (Granger) cause the explanatory variables, which are private final consumption expenditure, GFCF and personal disposable income and vice versa.

The bidirectional results suggest that remittances Granger cause per capita income. This implies that as remittances rise, it (Granger) cause per capita incomes to rise. Results also show that remittances Granger cause private consumption expenditure and personal disposable income at 2-year lags, while it Granger causes GFCF with 4-year lag.

These results indicate that remittances lead to an increase in per capita income, personal disposable incomes, private consumption expenditures and private investments. However, this impact may occur after a lag of 2–4 years. Rise in per capita income, private disposable incomes, private consumption expenditures and private investments is indicative of decline in poverty ratio. Since remittances directly reach the poor, the probability of remittances improving the living standards of poor and pulling them out of poverty is high.

Thus, these results together strongly indicate that remittances has had an impact on reducing poverty in India. GFCF does not Granger cause remittances, while per capita income, private consumption expenditure and personal disposable income Granger cause remittances. This is indicative of a two-way relationship between remittances and poverty.

Given the paucity of data, though a direct relationship could not be established between remittances and poverty, the results do indicate that remittances have contributed significantly to poverty-reducing indicators in India.

6.5 Impact of Remittances on Poverty in Kerala

6.5.1 Trends in Remittances and Poverty in Kerala

Kerala is one of the top remittance-receiving states of India. In 2008–2009, 20% of total emigrants from India were from Kerala. The state has witnessed a steadily growing trend in terms of emigrants (Fig. 6.3). However, the growth in inward remittances is much higher than the growth in emigrants. This indicates that more remittances are being sent per emigrant over time.

The movement of Keralites to almost all countries in the world has received much attention by the economists and the planners ever since large-scale emigration to the Gulf countries began in the 1970s as a consequence of oil boom. Though it would be interesting to examine the reasons for such high migration from this state and the rise in per capita remittances, we concentrate on the overall impact of remittances on the poverty indicators in the state.

Around 20% of total officially recorded remittances in India are received by Kerala. Many studies have pointed out that the dependence of people on remittances is very high in Kerala (e.g. Kannan and Hari 2002). In absolute terms, while the per capita net state domestic product (NSDP) rose by two times in the last two decades (1988–2008), the per capita remittances increased nearly 6 times during the same period. Comparison of remittances received by Kerala with all India shows that the trend growth of remittances during the period 1988–2008 registered 18.2% in Kerala as compared to 15.7% for all India.

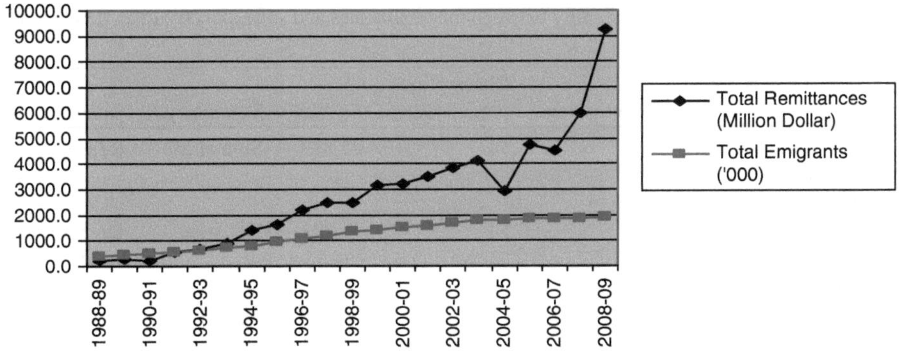

Fig. 6.3 Trends in emigrants and remittances in Kerala: 1988–1989 to 2008–2009 (Source: Total emigrants till 2002 is taken from 'Gulf Revisited Sept. 2004', CDS working paper no. 363, and the year after that is derived by adding the number of emigrant clearance data given by Ministry of Overseas Indian Affairs)

Remittances also seem to affect per capita consumption directly. This can be supported on the grounds that the per capita consumption in Kerala since 1977–1978 has grown much faster as compared to the national average without a corresponding increase in income. During the period 1988 to 2008, Kerala has witnessed an increase in annual average per capita NSDP by 5.8% against 14.7% increase of per capita remittances. At more disaggregate level, during the 1990s, the growth of remittances was much faster than the growth of Kerala's NSDP. The same holds true during the post-1990s too.

To assess the impact of remittances on poverty and its indicators in Kerala, we undertake Granger causality tests between remittances and per capita income and private consumption expenditure in Kerala. Given the paucity of data with respect to poverty ratio in the state (which is available with very long gaps), the direct relationship cannot be tested.

6.5.2 *Causality Between Remittances and Poverty-Related Indicators in Kerala*

Looking at high migration from Kerala over the last few decades, this section empirically estimates the impact of remittances on some key variables that affect poverty, namely, per capita income and private consumption expenditure in the state.

Using Granger causality test, we attempt to analyse how the remittances granger cause poverty-related indicators in the period 1990–2008. However, the limitation of the analysis is the low number of observations, which is 14 years. As explained earlier, this test critically depends on the number of lagged terms introduced in the model. The result is presented in Table 6.10. The null hypothesis

Table 6.10 Pairwise Granger causality between the remittances and some poverty-related indicators in Kerala

Direction of causality/ null hypothesis	Number of lags	Observations (no. of years)	F-Value	Significance	Decision
Remittance does not Granger cause per capita NSDP	4	14	27.883	Sign at 5%	Reject
Per capita NSDP does not Granger cause remittances	4	14	7.101	Not sign	Do not reject
Remittance does not Granger cause GFCF	2	13	4.669	Sign at 5%	Reject
GFCF does not Granger cause remittances	2	13	0.903	Not sign	Do not reject

Source: Authors estimation from the dataset

considered is that remittances do not Granger cause the explanatory variables and vice versa.

The results show that remittances Granger cause per capita income in the state. The results also show that per capita income does not Granger cause remittances. This result is similar to that arrived for remittances and per capita income at all India level. Undertaking the test for remittances and gross fixed capital formation (GFCF), it is found that remittances Granger cause GFCF, while GFCF does not Granger cause remittances. The results therefore indicate that higher remittances in Kerala have led to higher per capita income and higher investments. These indicators are closely linked with poverty. Similar results are found by other studies on Kerala. For example, Srivastava (2003) highlighted that in Kerala, remittances constituted 21% of state income in the 1990s. This flow appears to have increased wealth; although the average per capita consumption in Kerala was below the national average until 1978–1979, by 1999–2000 consumer expenditure in Kerala exceeded the national average by around 41%.

Empirical evidence therefore suggests that remittances have played a significant role in Kerala's economy by increasing per capita income and investments and to that extent may have contributed in reducing poverty levels.

6.6 Conclusions and Policy Recommendations

The benefits of remittances, as financial flows to the developing countries, are well documented in the literature. Remittances are more stable and predictable as compared to other financial flows, and more importantly, they are countercyclical providing buffer against economic shocks. In conflict or post-conflict situations, remittances can be crucial to survival, sustenance, rehabilitation and reconstruction. However, impact of remittances on poverty has led to a considerable debate. Studies that argue against remittances having poverty-reducing effect point out that given the high transaction costs of migrating, 'truly poor' do not migrate. While this argument has some merit, it has little evidential support as a stream of studies from different countries has shown that 'very poor' and 'poor' do migrate.[13]. Further, the average annual growth of remittances to low-income countries in the period 2004–2008 was 22%, which was higher than to middle-income countries (18.9%).

Apart from the debate on whether poor migrate or not, there is a growing debate, with little empirical evidence, on whether remittances is able to effectively reduce poverty levels in the recipient country or not. To address this issue, a case study on India, which is one of the top recipients of remittances, has been undertaken, and impact of remittances on poverty measures has been estimated. Further, the impact of remittances on poverty, in top remittance-receiving state of India, namely, Kerala, has also been estimated.

With respect to India, empirical estimates show that a 10% rise in remittances as a share of GDP leads to 1.7% reduction in poverty ratio. The Granger causality tests indicate that remittances have affected some key variables that are directly linked with poverty. These are per capita income, private consumption expenditure, personal disposable income and gross fixed capital formation or investments. For Kerala (where remittances constitute 21% of state domestic product), Granger causality tests show that remittances Granger cause rise in per capita income and investments.

Though the empirical evidence indicates that remittances can reduce poverty in the recipient countries, what makes remittances work for poverty reduction is not clear. There are many factors affecting this channel. To begin with, remittances are a function of the numbers of migrants, the amount of money they earn and their propensity to remit. However, migrants may have large propensity to remit, but the home and host country policies may not be conducive to remittances. Even if the policies are conducive, due to absence of appropriate channels of sending remittances, these may reach the poor only after a long gap (when the migrant decides to carry the remittances personally or sent it through someone). This may not be very effective in terms of reducing poverty. Even if poor receive the remittances, proper use of remittances is important for sustainable reduction in poverty.

Given the number of facilitating factors required for remittances to work for poor, it is unlikely for it to happen on its own. Sustained policy intervention at each

[13] Sabates Wheeler, Sabates and Castaldo (2005).

stage is required. To begin with, migration has to be accepted as a win-win situation by origin and destination countries. Migrants contribute to the development of home country in a number of ways including remittances and to development of host country by filling the labour demand and supply gap. It is therefore important to view migration as pro-development by all. However, in order to receive migrants that fill the demand and supply gap in the migrant-receiving countries, international fora may be used to formulate policy frameworks to facilitate the flow of migrants and reduce the number of irregular migrants.

Higher social security of migrants is likely to increase their propensity to remit. However, a substantial part of remittances depends on informal channels like physical carriage by trustworthy relatives, friends or migrants themselves. Reasons for preferring informal channels for remittances include considerations of cost, speed, ease of making and receiving the transfer, coverage within the home country and greater confidence and trust in the service provided. However, these channels are slow, cumbersome, costly and not entirely risk-free. The ability to remit money at one node of an existing national network and receiving the money at another node can make huge difference in improving the cost efficiency and ease of sending remittances. National networks like post offices, which are present throughout the country, in both origin and destination countries, can be used and special networks can be developed for remittances.

The International Development Committee (2003–2004) has outlined a number of schemes offered by different developing countries to encourage remittances. Some of these schemes include higher interest rates for foreign currency accounts like those offered by India, Pakistan and Bangladesh; 'three plus one' matching funds scheme offered by the Zacatecas State Government in Mexico in which every dollar remitted by a Mexican migrant worker to their Home Town Association is matched with three more, one from the municipality, one from the state and one from the federal government; and use of bonds issued with future flows of migrants' remittances used as collateral as done by Brazil.

Efforts to increase the volume of remittances should also be supported by efforts in channelling the remittances to more productive uses for sustainable reduction in poverty. Apart from providing food security to the households, if remittances are used for improving skills and productivity of the recipients, they will have more sustainable impact on improvements of standard of living. Families receiving remittances should be allowed to use future remittances as collateral for procuring loans for education, house building or other activities like procuring fertilizers and machinery for farms. Remittances if channelized in the right direction can be an important instrument in reducing poverty in developing countries.

Acknowledgement This chapter is based on UNCTAD-India Study on 'Impact of Remittances on Poverty in Developing Countries', published by UNCTAD, 2011.

Appendix 1

Using time-series data from 1973–1974 to 2007–2008, the unit root test is undertaken to examine the stationarity of the dataset. The stationarity of variables such as remittances, GDP, poverty ratio, GFCF, personal disposable income and private final consumption expenditure has been checked for the available 28 years dataset. For the said purpose, the augmented Dickey-Fuller (ADF) and Phillips-Perron (PP) test is used. The ADF is conducted by adding the lagged values of the dependent variables. The idea is to include enough lag terms so that the error term in the equation is serially uncorrelated. Here, while testing the ADF and the PP test, the null and the alternative hypothesis is that, when $b_0 = 0$, the series is non-stationary and when $b_0 < 0$ then the series is stationary.

The ADF test is obtained by using the following format of the equation:

$$\delta x_t = a_0 + b_0 x_{t-1} + \sum_{i=1}^{k} C_0 \, \delta x_{t-1} + w_t$$

where δ is the difference operator, $\alpha_{0,}$ b_0 and c_0 are the coefficients to be estimated, x is the variable whose time-series operators are examined and w is the white noise error term. The results are reported in following tables.

Appendix 1.1 Stationary Test of the Following Variables: ADF Test and Phillips-Perron (Kerala)

Variables	Aug. Dickey-Fuller test	*t*-Statistics	Remarks
Per capita NSDP	ADF test statistics	*−4.522****	Per capita NSDP was not stationary at level and first difference. It is observed stationary at second difference
	1% level	−3.887	
	5% level	−3.052	
	10% level	−2.667	
Remittances	ADF test statistics	*−4.299***	Remittances were found stationary at level
	1% level	−4.533	
	5% level	−3.674	
	10% level	−3.277	
Per capita NSDP	Phillips-Perron test		Per capita NSDP was not stationary at level and first difference. It is observed stationary at second difference
	Phil.-P statistics	*−18.567****	
	1% level	−3.959	
	5% level	−3.081	
	10% level	−2.681	

(continued)

(continued)

Variables	Aug. Dickey-Fuller test	*t*-Statistics	Remarks
Remittances	Phil.-P statistics	−4.299**	Remittances were found stationary at level
	1% level	−4.533	
	5% level	−3.674	
	10% level	−3.277	

Appendix 1.2 Stationary Test of the Following Variables: ADF Test (All India)

Variables	Aug. Dickey-Fuller test	*t*-Statistics	Remarks
Remittances	ADF test statistics	*−8.2695****	FDI was not stationary at level, first difference. It is observed stationary at second difference
	1% level	−4.3561	
	5% level	−3.595	
	10% level	−3.2335	
GDP	ADF test statistics	*−3.3917**	GDP was not stationary at level, but observed stationary at first difference
	1% level	−4.324	
	5% level	−3.5806	
	10% level	−3.2253	
GFCF	ADF test statistics	*−6.3119****	GFCF was not stationary at level, first difference. It is observed stationary at second difference
	1% level	−4.3561	
	5% level	−3.595	
	10% level	−3.2335	
Disp. income	ADF test statistics	*−5.8736****	Disposable income was not stationary at level, first difference. It is observed stationary at second difference
	1% level	−4.3743	
	5% level	−3.6032	
	10% level	−3.2381	
Pvt. final consumption exp	ADF test statistics	*−4.4596****	Disposable income was not stationary at level, but it was found stationary at first difference
	1% level	−4.3393	
	5% level	−3.5875	
	10% level	−3.2292	

Note: * and *** represent the significance level at 10 and 1% level

Interestingly all the variables under consideration are found non-stationary at levels. In other words, it shows that the past results cannot be used to predict future results of any variables. This is because the non-stationary in the data reveals that the mean and the variance do not remain constant over time. However, the variables such as GDP and private final consumption expenditure are found stationary when they are first differenced, whereas all other variables become stationary at second difference. The level of significance for ADF statistics for all variables is at one percentage level except GDP (at 10% level). Appendix-1.3 reports results of Phillips-Perron (PP) test.

Appendix 1.3 Stationary Test of the Following Variables: Phillips-Perron Test (All India)

	Phillips-Perron		
Variables		*t*-Statistics	Remarks
Remittances	Phil-Perron test stat	*−8.8452****	FDI was not stationary at level, first difference. It is observed stationary at second difference
	1% level	−4.3561	
	5% level	−3.595	
	10% level	−3.2335	
GDP	Phil-Perron test stat	*−3.37**	GDP was not stationary at level, but observed stationary at first difference
	1% level	−4.324	
	5% level	−3.5806	
	10% level	−3.2253	
GFCF	Phil-Perron test stat	*−6.6006****	GFCF was not stationary at level, first difference. It is observed stationary at second difference
	1% level	−4.3561	
	5% level	−3.595	
	10% level	−3.2335	
Disp. income	Phil-Perron test stat	*−4.5374****	Disposable income was not stationary at level but it was found stationary at first difference
	1% level	−4.3393	
	5% level	−3.5875	
	10% level	−3.2292	
Pvt. final consumption exp.	Phil-Perron test stat	*−4.4997****	Disposable income was not stationary at level but it was found stationary at first difference
	1% level	−4.3393	
	5% level	−3.5875	
	10% level	−3.2292	

Note: * and *** represent the significance level at 10 and 1% level

The results show that, on using the Phillips-Perron (PP) test the variables such as GDP, personal disposable income and private final consumption expenditure are found stationary when they are first differenced, whereas other variables become stationary at second difference.

References

Adams R, Jr (2005a) Remittances, selection bias and poverty in Guatemala. Unpublished Manuscript. World Bank, Washington, DC

Adams R, Page J (2005) Do international migration and remittances reduce poverty in developing countries? World Dev 33(10):1645–1669

Adelman I, Edward Taylor J (1990) Is structural adjustment with a human face possible? The case of Mexico. J Dev Stud 26(3):387–407

Barjas A, Chami R, Fullenkamp C, Gapen M, Montiel P (2009) Do workers' remittances promote economic growth?. IMF Working Paper 153/2009

Bouhga-Hagbe J (2004) A theory of workers remittance with an application to Morocco. IMF working paper no 04/194, Washington, DC

Campos R, de Palomo L (2002) Invirtamos en Educación para Desafiar el Crecimiento Económico y la Pobreza. Fundación Salvadoreña para el Desarrollo Económico y Social, San Salvador, May

Chami R, Fullenkamp C, Jahjah S (2005) Are immigrant remittance flows a source of capital for development. IMF Staff Pap, Palgrave Macmillan 52(1):55–81

Chimhowu AO, Piesse J, Pinder C (2005) The socio-economic impact of remittances on poverty reduction. In: Maimbo SM, Ratha D (eds) Remittances: development, impact and future prospects. The World Bank, Washington, DC

Cox-Edwards A, Rodríguez Oreggia E (2009) Remittance and labor force participation in mexico: an analysis using propensity score matching. World Develop 37(5):1004–1014

Drinkwater S, P Levine, E Lotti (2003) The labour market effects of remittances. FLOWENLA discussion paper no. 6. Hamburg Institute of International Economics, Hamburg

Durand J, Parrado EA, Massey DS (1996) Migradollars and development: a reconsideration of the Mexican case. Int Migr Rev 30(2):423–444

Ekanayake EM, Halkides M (2008) Do remittances and foreign direct investment promote growth? Evidence from developing countries. J Int Bus Econ 8(1)

Faini R (2002) Development, trade, and migration. Revue d'Économie et du Développement. In: Proceedings from the ABCDE Europe conference, 1–2, pp 85–116

Faini R (2003) The Brain drain: an unmitigated blessing? Centro Studi Luca d'Agliano Development Studies working paper no. 173

Frank R (2001) Philippine Town Plies a road to Riches via Monthly Stipends: but are Pozorrubians turning into Slakers as relatives abroad send home cash? Wall Street Journal, 22 May

Funkhouser E (1992) Migration from Nicaragua: some recent evidence. World Develop 20(8):1209–1218

Gustafsson B, Makonnen N (1993) Poverty and remittances in Lesotho. J Afr Econ 2:49–73

Hildebrandt N, McKenzie D (2005) The effects of migration on child health in Mexico. Economica 6(1):257–289

IMF (2005) World economic outlook. International Monetary Fund, Washington, DC

Kannan KP, Hari KS (2002) Kerala's gulf connection emigration, remittances and their macroeconomic impact 1972–2000. Working paper no. 328, CDS, Kerala

Lopez Cordova JE (2005) Globalization, migration, and development: the role of Mexican migrant remittances. Economía 6(1):217–256

McCormick B, Wahba J (2001) Overseas work experiences, saving and entrepreneurship amongst return migrants to LCDs. Scott J Polit Econ 48:164–178

Pant B (2008) Mobilizing remittances for productive use: a policy-oriented approach. Nepal Rastra Bank, working paper serial number: NRB/WP/4, Dec 2008

Pindyck RS, Rubinfeld DL (1998) Econometric models and economic forecasts, 4th edn. McGraw Hill Book Co., New York

Rajan RG, Subramanyam A (2005) What undermines growth impact on growth? IMF working paper no. 05/126, Washington, DC

Rapoport H, Docquier F (2006) The economics of migrants' remittances. In: Kolm SC, Ythier JM (eds) Handbook of the economics of giving, altruism and reciprocity: volume 2. North-Holland, Amsterdam, pp 1135–1199

Ratha D (2003) Workers' Remittances: an important and stable source of external development finance. In: Global development finance 2003. World Bank, Washington, DC

Ravallion M (1997) Can high-inequality developing countries escape absolute poverty? Econ Lett 56:51–57

Ravallion M, Chen S (1997) What can new survey data tell us about recent changes in distribution and poverty? World Bank Econ Rev 11(2):357–382

Rodriguez ER, Tiongson ER (2001) Temporary migration overseas and household labour supply: evidence from urban Philippines. Int Migr Rev 35:3

Sabates-Wheeler R, Sabates R, Castaldo A (2005) Tackling poverty-migration linkages: evidence from Ghana and Egypt. Working Paper WP-T14, Migration DRC. University of Sussex, UK

Spatafora N (2005) Two current issues facing developing countries, Chapter Two. In: World economic outlook: a survey by the staff of the International Monetary Fund

Taylor JE, Mora J, Adams R (2005) Remittances, inequality and poverty: evidence from Rural Mexico. Unpublished manuscript. University of California, Davis

Uruci E, GedeshI I (2003) Remittances management in Albania. CeSPI working paper, 5/2003

Woodruff C, Zenteno R (2001) Remittances and micro-enterprises in Mexico. In: Global economic prospects. World Bank, Washington, DC

World Bank (2006) Global economic prospects: economic implications and migration. World Bank, Washington, DC

Yang D (2004) International migration, human capital, and entrepreneurship: evidence from Philippine migrants' exchange rate shocks. Working papers 531, Research Seminar in International Economics, University of Michigan

Chapter 7
Understanding NREGA: A Simple Theory and Some Facts

Diganta Mukherjee and Uday Bhanu Sinha

7.1 Introduction

The policy of employment guarantee scheme (EGS) is well known since the 1817 Poor Employment Act and the 1834 Poor Law Amendment Act in Great Britain (Blaug 1963, 1964), and the New Deal programmes of the 1930s in the United States (Kesselman 1978; Bernstein 1970), and it was considered an important element of relief policies during natural disasters and economic downturns. In recent past, this kind of schemes were followed both in developed and developing countries with multiple objectives such as poverty reduction, building and maintaining public infrastructure and improving bargaining power of the workers. Among others, some notable examples of such schemes mainly for poverty alleviation are as followed by Chile (1987), India (1978), Pakistan (1992), Bangladesh (1983), Philippines (1990), Botswana (1960) and Kenya (1992).

The EGS is a policy of direct transfer to the poor through the provision of public works (Drèze and Sen 1991; Lipton 1996; von Braun 1995) satisfying the property of self-selection (Besley and Coate 1992; Besley and Kanbur 1993), and the magnitude of such direct transfer benefits was empirically studied (Ravallion 1991; Ravallion et al. 1993). The earlier studies on rural public works programmes emphasised its role as income insurance in the presence of seasonality in agrarian labour market (Basu 2007), for building longer-term capital assets (Basu 1981), preventing dislocation of families in search of jobs and food (Drèze and Sen 1991), affecting rural-urban migration (Ravallion 1990).

D. Mukherjee
Indian Statistical Institute, Kolkata, India
e-mail: digantam@hotmail.com

U.B. Sinha (✉)
Department of Economics, Delhi School of Economics,
University of Delhi, New Delhi 110007, India
e-mail: uday@econdse.org

N.S. Siddharthan and K. Narayanan (eds.), *Human Capital and Development: The Indian Experience*, DOI 10.1007/978-81-322-0857-0_7, © Springer India 2013

Though the policy of employment guarantee schemes is commonly followed by governments in both developing and developed countries alike as a relief policy, there is very little by way of formal theoretical modelling to understand the issue. Recently, Basu et al. (2010) provided a theoretical framework to analyse both the positive and normative implications of such a policy in a spectrum of labour market structures. While the introduction of such a scheme introduces a contestability in the labour market where government is another employer, however, the outcome with respect to wages and overall level of employment in the labour market would depend on the "degree of distributional and/or efficiency concerns of the planner". In this chapter, we analyse the impact of NREGA scheme on (1) rural labour market, (2) income of the poor households and (3) overall agricultural production. When the income from NREGA alone can be a substantial part of the target income of the poor, the poor may exhibit a backward-bending supply curve of labour which may lead to an aggregate reduction in agricultural output. This adverse production effect can happen even when the NREGA activities lead to a moderate improvement in agricultural productivity.

Consider the scenario where there exists a labour market with demand and supply of labour and a wage rate. Even if the wage is competitively determined, it may not be adequate for the poor household to reach their target income, what they consider as means of a decent living for their households. Envisaging situations like these, the Indian government from time to time has implemented different policies to complement the income of the poor. The National Rural Employment Guarantee Act (NREGA) is one such policy of EGS which is introduced in recent past. Passed by the Lok Sabha on 23 August 2004, and signed by the President of India on 5 September 2005, NREGA has been hailed as a major initiative in the government of India's commitment to providing an economic safety net to India's rural poor. The NREGA extends to all rural areas of India, including fifth and sixth schedule areas, except the state of Jammu and Kashmir. In this chapter, we would provide a conceptual framework and also some empirical facts for understanding the different plausible impacts of NREGA. Some of the impacts have already been documented by different studies (see Mathur 2007; Mehrotra 2008). In the following subsections, we first outline the scope of the scheme and the debate that surrounds it.

7.1.1 *The Scheme: National Rural Employment Guarantee Act of India, 2005*[1]

Data show that 71.9% of India's population still resides in rural areas (2002), and given that the majority of India's poor also resides in rural areas, the NREGA can be thought of as a policy to boost rural income, stabilise agricultural production and reduce the population pressure in urban areas through migration.

[1] This section borrows from Basu et al. (2005).

Some of the original provisions of the NREGA were as outlined below:

1. Every household in the rural areas of India shall have a right to at least 100 days of guaranteed employment every year for at least one adult member, for doing casual manual labour at the rate of Rs. 60 per day.
2. Only productive works shall be taken up under the programme. The State Council shall prepare a list of permissible works as well as a list of "preferred works". The identification of preferred works shall be based on the economic, social and environmental benefits of different types of works, their contribution to social equity and their ability to create permanent assets.
3. The programme may also provide, as far as possible, for the training and upgradation of the skills of unskilled labourers.
4. Wages may be paid in cash or in kind or both, taking into account the guidelines and recommendations of the State Council on this matter as far as possible.
5. Employment shall be provided within a radius of 5 km of the village where the applicant resides at the time of applying. In cases where employment is provided outside such radius, it must be provided within the block and transport allowances and daily living allowances shall be paid in accordance with programme rules.
6. In cases where at least 20 women are employed on a worksite, a provision shall be made for one of them to be deputed to look after any children under the age of six who may be brought to the worksite, if the need arises. The person deputed for child minding shall be paid the statutory minimum wage.
7. A proportion of the wages, not exceeding 5%, may be deducted as a contribution to welfare schemes organised for the benefit of labourers employed under the programme, such as health insurance, accident insurance, survivor benefits, maternity benefits and social security schemes.[2]

The NREGA scheme also comes with two important riders:

1. Public works programmes should not compete with agricultural labour hiring decisions.
2. Public works programmes should generate a productive asset that directly impacts agricultural productivity.

However, with most of Indian agriculture characterised by seasonality – a lean season when agricultural labour demand is low and a harvest season when labour demand is high – it was reasonably assumed that the public employment, guaranteed for at least 100 days, will be instituted during the lean season when the rural

[2] There are eight specific types of works listed in the NREGA: (1) water conservation and water harvesting; (2) drought proofing including afforestation; (3) irrigation canals; (4) provision of irrigation facility to land owned by SC and ST, and land of beneficiaries of land reforms and of Indira Awaas Yojana (IAY) (rural housing for poor); (5) renovation of traditional water bodies; (6) land development; (7) flood control works; (8) rural connectivity to provide all weather access; and (9) any other work, which may be notified by central government in consultation with state government (see Mehrotra 2008 for more discussion on this issue).

labour force is most vulnerable. Some of the performance parameters of the scheme are illustrated in Table 7.1, where we outline the spread of the programme in different states of the country, in terms of number of districts covered, funds and its utilisation, coverage in terms of man-days and number of households covered. The general pattern of these performance indicators remains stable even up to 2010–2011.[3]

7.1.2 The Debate

NREGA is supposed to alleviate rural poverty, but the operational dimensions of the NREGA have been subject to much debate regarding the efficacy and targeting of the act. NREGA has attracted mixed reactions from economists and policy analysts.[4] There has been considerable discussion on whether the employment has been successfully targeted to the poor or there are leakages to those above the poverty line. The most detailed evaluation so far has been undertaken by Dreze and Khera (2009), covering six states in 2007–2008. Dreze and Khera (2009) find that 98% of the sample workers stated that they were ready to work for 100 days in the year – the "upper limit" under the Act. NREGA as of now meets only a fraction of this demand: in their survey only 13% of the respondents had actually secured 100 days of NREGA work in the preceding 12 months. There are, of course, wide interstate variations in this respect. While the proportion of sample workers who had completed 100 days of work was particularly low in Chhattisgarh (1%), Bihar (2%), Uttar Pradesh (3%) and Jharkhand (7%), it was considerably higher in Madhya Pradesh (17%) and as high as 35% in Rajasthan. Also see Table 7.2, columns 7 and 8, for a state-wise breakdown of employment provided (person-days). The numbers are all well below the target. Again, checking more recent data (updated till 2010–2011) reveals small improvement in performance.

We start with the presumption that rural labour markets in India do not conform to the classic competitive labour markets of economics textbooks. If they did, the arguments for the NREGA would be weaker. In fact, the labour market in rural India can best be characterised as imperfect with high costs on the part of workers to seek and to switch employment, and with elements of collusion and social power on the part of employer that lead to low wages, and above all to equilibrium unemployment.

Assuming the NREGA targets this group of unemployed workers, the possibility of an alternative source of income raises the reservation wage of all workers in the rural sector, and implicitly confers some bargaining power to rural

---

[3] All the data cited in this chapter are from the relevant government of India websites like http://www.agricoop.nic.in/ and http://nrega.nic.in/netnrega/home.aspx. Further calculations are done by authors.

[4] Much has been written about NREGA both in favour and against the programme. Some argued that the NREGA was unnecessary because in any case poor agricultural workers had a very low unemployment rate (*Business Standard*, 25 December 2004).

Table 7.1 Some performance parameters for states and districts, 2006–2007

State	No. of NREGA districts	Funds available (Rs in cr)	Expen-diture	Percentage utilised	Average person days (in lakh)per district	Daily unskilled wage paid (Rs)	% Of households completed 100 days of employment	
							2006–2007	2007–2008
Andhra Pradesh	13	1142	680	59.6	52	86	2.7	9
Assam	7	707		83.7	82	67	23.4	17.1
Bihar	23	1197	713	59.8	26	70	3.6	0.7
Chhattisgarh	11	841	669	79.5	64	63	10.4	11.2
Gujarat	6	124	85	69.4	17	56	5.4	3.9
Haryana	2	47	36	77.3	12	97	11.1	10.4
Himachal Pradesh	2	57	39	68.9	15	69	26.5	5.1
Jammu and Kashmir	3	50	35	68.9	11	69	9.7	1.4
Jharkhand	20	982	712	72.4	26	80	3.7	3
Karnataka	6	341	248	72.8	37	67	12.8	4.2
Kerala	2	48	28	57.7	10	121	0.5	32.1
Madhya Pradesh	18	2134	1862	87.3	110	59	18.5	21
Maharashtra	10	630	395	62.6	44	70	1.5	1.8
Meghalaya	2	26		81.7	12.1	73	0.6	6.4
Mizoram	2	26		63.2	3.9	175	11.7	0
Orissa	19	890	733	82.4	42	53	11.1	3.4
Punjab	1	38	25	65.1	11	96	16.8	5.3
Rajasthan	6	856	693	81	167	51	54.4	42
Sikkim	1	5		57.4	2.4	87	5.4	10.2
Tamil Nadu	6	252	151	60.2	31	80	0.3	6.2
Tripura	1	50		90.6	50	60	26.3	0.4
Uttar Pradesh	22	1029	780	75.8	37	56	6	10.9
Uttarakhand	3	71	48	68.3	13	72	2.8	8.3
West Bengal	12	486	174	35.9	13	104	0.6	0.8
All India	200	12073	8823	73	90.51cr	65	10.2	10.8

Table 7.2 Importance of NREGA wage in pushing families above poverty line

State	Rural poverty line	Poor % age	Poor persons lakhs	Avg. Agri. wage, men	NREGA wage	Employment provided –number of person-days per household		NREGA income	Pov annual income, family of 4	NREGA/ Pov. ratio	Pov annual income, family of 5	NREGA/ Pov. ratio
						2006–2007	2007–2008					
Andhra Pradesh	292.95	11.2	64.7	36.61	80	31.4	39.6	8,000	14061.60	56.89	17577.00	45.51
Assam	387.64	22.3	54.5	30.23	66	72.5	34.7	6,600	18606.72	35.47	23258.40	28.38
Bihar	354.36	42.1	336.72	45.06	77	35.3	21.1	7,700	17009.28	45.27	21261.60	36.22
Gujarat	353.93	19.1	63.49	55.48	50	43.7	29.6	5,000	16988.64	29.43	21235.80	23.55
Haryana	414.76	13.6	21.49	57.83	99.21	48.2	50	9,921	19908.48	49.83	24885.60	39.87
Himachal Pradesh	394.28	10.7	6.14	12.95	75	49.8	35.9	7,500	18925.44	39.63	23656.80	31.70
Jammu and Kashmir	391.26	4.6	3.66	31.82	70	26.9	31.7	7,000	18780.48	37.27	23475.60	29.82
Karnataka	324.17	20.8	75.05	49	74	41.1	44.4	7,400	15560.16	47.56	19450.20	38.05
Kerala	430.12	13.2	32.43	55.89	125	22.8	28.6	12,500	20645.76	60.55	25807.20	48.44
Madhya Pradesh	327.78	36.9	175.65	40.61	67	68.9	63.3	6,700	15733.44	42.58	19666.80	34.07
Maharashtra	362.25	29.6	171.13	52.97	69	40.8	39	6,900	17388.00	39.68	21735.00	31.75
Orissa	325.79	46.8	151.75	44.86	70	57.5	37	7,000	15637.92	44.76	19547.40	35.81
Punjab	410.38	9.1	15.12	32.01	94.48	52	10.5	9,448	19698.24	47.96	24622.80	38.37
Rajasthan	374.57	18.7	87.38	44.16	73	85.4	75	7,300	17979.36	40.60	22474.20	32.48
Tamil Nadu	351.86	22.8	76.5	60.79	80	26.9	57.2	8,000	16889.28	47.37	21111.60	37.89
Uttar Pradesh	365.84	33.4	473	47.79	100	32	33.1	10,000	17560.32	56.95	21950.40	45.56
West Bengal	382.82	28.6	173.22	44.58	70	14.3	22.5	7,000	18375.36	38.09	22969.20	30.48
All India	356.30	28.3	2209.24			43.1	41.8					

workers. Thus, it is clear that the fact of a guarantee of employment at a given wage through the NREGA would introduce *contestability* in the rural labour market. In other words, in the presence of NREGA scheme, the large land holders in rural areas may now need to raise wage of workers they hire in order to ensure the necessary supply of labour.

The key questions are whether the NREGA can have fruitful impact on poverty, raise private sector wages and overall employment for rural labour force. Will it lead to higher aggregate production? The answers essentially lie in how the labour supply schedule available to large land holders in agriculture react to the opposing effects of the NREGA. On the one hand, the NREGA scheme provides an alternative source of employment which may lead to a reduction in the pool of workers available for private employer in a particular year, and also the potential contestability effect of the NREGA in terms of higher wage reduces the demand for labour in private employment; on the other hand, there is positive effect in terms of higher productivity in agriculture. Though the eventual outcome is more of a matter of empirical investigation, but here in this chapter we would provide some theoretical predictions with the help of a baseline model.[5]

We outline a simple theoretical model for the above discussions in the following section looking at the (im)perfection of the labour market and the effect of NREGA in the rural labour supply decision. We go on to discuss the aggregate production consequences, considering alternative productivity implications of the scheme in Sect. 7.3. In Sect. 7.4, we provide some empirical evidence in support of our concerns highlighted in the theoretical framework. Section 7.5 concludes with some future directions of research.

7.2 A Simple Theoretical Model

Consider a rural economy with two types of households: rich and poor. There are m number of rich households and n number of poor households (reasonably, we assume that $m<n$). Each household has L number of labour days available in a year. The rich household has enough land (K) in their disposal, and as a result, they would like to employ more labour from outside the household at a reasonable wage. Therefore, they would be net buyer of labour service. On the other hand, the poor household has little land to work with ($k<K$) and, as a result, each poor household has excess supply of labour which they can sell in the market. The agricultural production functions for both rich and poor households are the same. $Q=f(\cdot)$ is a function of land and labour, and it is only the endowment of land that is different. Given that there is not much sales and purchase of land happening in rural India, we assume

[5] The productive value of NREGA works is also something of a mystery. The general impression is that they are mostly useless. Some dismissed them as a futile attempt "to play with mud, to create a road that goes from nowhere to nowhere, to dig ditches that will be washed away in the next monsoon" (*The Hindustan Times*, 14 February 2008). This verdict, however, is hard to substantiate or negate, and we leave this again as a subject of empirical enquiry.

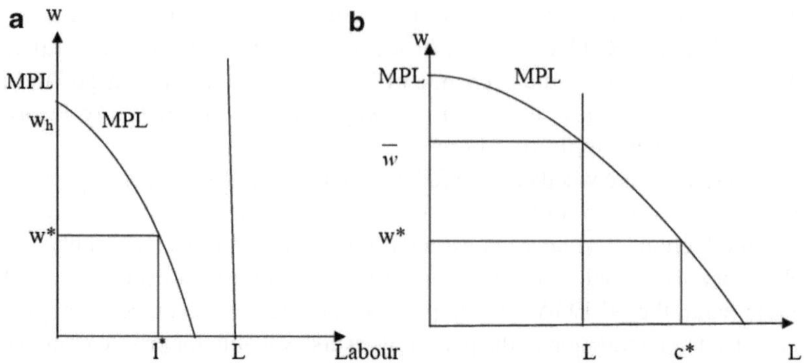

Fig. 7.1 (**a**) Poor household's own employment. (**b**) Rich household's own employment (L), and thus MPL to the *right* of L is the labour demand cure of the rich households

that land market does not exist and each household whether rich or poor has fixed amount of land which is part of the inherited property.[6]

Thus, the rich household has the production $f(K, \cdot)$ and the poor household has the production $f(k, \cdot)$ depending on their choice of employment of labour. Given the fixed endowment of land, the production function satisfies the usual properties of first and second derivatives with respect to labour. That is, the marginal productivity of labour is positive and downward-sloping curve. However, keeping in view the features of agricultural production process, we take the marginal productivity curve of labour to attain zero after some labour employment on any fixed plot of land.[7]

7.2.1 Perfect Labour Market

Given the production function, in perfect labour market without a friction, the equilibrium wage would be established at a wage where the total supply of labour from the poor household is equal to the total demand for labour from the rich household. Define the equilibrium wage as w* (Fig. 7.1).

At w^* the poor household employs an amount of labour say l^* in their own land. So the excess labour supply they have is $L-l^*$. Thus, the total supply of labour would be $n(L-l^*)$. At w^* suppose the rich wants to employ c^* amount of lbaour (given the marginal productivity of labour on their land). Out of c^* the rich employs their own supply L, and any additional labour they need they demand it from the market. Thus, the demand for labour for the rich household at w^* is c^*-L per

[6] Basu et al. (2010) found in their sample that 94% of land is inherited, while 2% is purchased, and the rest of land is obtained either as gifts or through share cropping or through encroachment of village commons or forests.

[7] The standard textbook in Development Economics always work with such a scenario (for instance, see Basu (1997) and Ray (1998)).

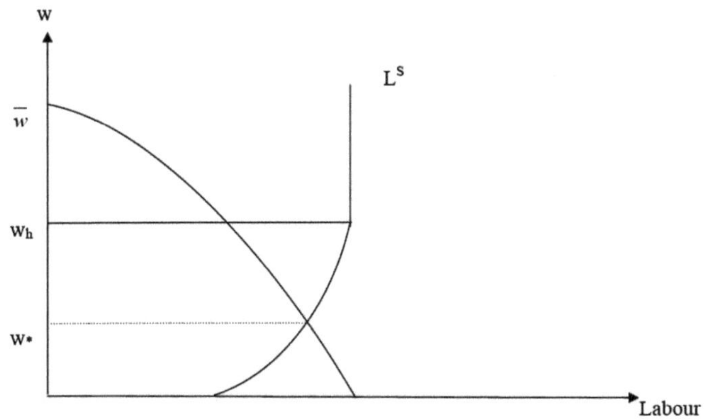

Fig. 7.2 Equilibrium in the perfect labour market (Demand for and supply of labour)

household. Therefore, the total demand for labour for the rich households would be $m(c^* - L)$. In the perfect labour market w^* would be such that

$$n\left(L-1^*\right)=m\left(c^*-L\right). \tag{7.1}$$

It is clear from the behaviour of the marginal productivity of labour curves that RHS is a decreasing function of w and the LHS is an increasing function of w. With some additional regularity assumptions, it is possible that competitive labour market equilibrium exists and it would be obtained at a unique wage level w^*.

Given the labour demand of the rich household and the supply of labour of the poor household, we draw (in Fig. 7.2) the market demand and supply of labour which is the horizontal sum of the demand for labour from all rich households and the supply of all poor households.

If the equilibrium wage is above some w_h, then the poorer household would stop their own cultivation and supply the entire labour force for the cultivation of the rich households. But given the current scenario where $m << n$, this is unlikely to happen. Also, if m is so low that w^* is driven down to zero, then due to biological subsistence restrictions, the prevailing subsistence wage will be greater than the market-clearing wage. There will be unemployment as the people willing to work would not receive the employment due to lack of demand from the rich households. This excess labour would naturally work on their own land and might even drive the marginal productivity of their family cultivation to zero. Thus, we will have a situation of labour surplus economy.

On the other hand, we may have a well-functioning perfect labour market when the demand and supply intersect at a reasonable wage above subsistence and the equilibrium is obtained at w^*. For the labour market to function, we need that (1) the demand and supply of labour curves are well behaved and (2) they have an intersection at a positive wage above subsistence wage. In order to achieve such well-behaved demand and supply curves, it must be the case that both types of household maximise their income, and also the utility is a monotonically *strictly increasing* function of income for both types of household. In order to ensure the intersection in the relevant economic range of wages, the population of rich and poor should be in certain proportion. As mentioned above, if there are too many poor household as compared to rich we will have labour surplus economy.

It is possible to have a situation where even though the labour market is perfect and we have an equilibrium wage determined by the market forces of demand and supply, the poor households may not receive adequate income in order to maintain a decent living or else at least maintain a living above the relevant poverty line of income.

It is obvious that when a programme like NREGA is introduced in a perfectly functioning labour market and assuming that NREGA work is preferred over working for the rich households at all wages, then the supply curve of the labour would shift leftward, leading to a higher market-clearing wage. In such a situation the poor and rich household would employ less labour for agricultural cultivation. As a result, the total agricultural production will fall.[8] On the other hand, if there is surplus labour in the economy and in case the NREGA works are provided just to absorb that surplus labour, then there may not be any adverse effect on agricultural production. Of course, this prediction is based on the assumption that NREGA works are not creating any permanent asset which can impinge on the productivity of land.

7.2.2 Imperfect Labour Market

It has been revealed by various studies undertaken in rural India that the labour market is not perfect and the wages are typically suppressed far below the competitive wage due to the presence of extra-economic coercion and other factors such as feudal forces exerted by the rich households or caste. Also, in some regions due to population pressure, the prevailing wages as well as the works available are not adequate for the poor households for a sustainable living which often leads to large scale migration. Thus, the existence of surplus labour in agriculture at the prevailing wage is a feature of labour market which does not go well with the assumption of perfect labour market.[9]

Consider that all poor households have a target level of income, say T. T can well be interpreted as the poverty line or a level of income which the poor household aspires to achieve for their decent living. In other words, this can be interpreted as

[8] This relies on the assumption that substitution of labour by machine is not possible in the short run. However, there are evidences that the demand for labour saving technology such as tractors and harvesters has gone up in response to NREGA in some states like Haryana and Punjab in India.

[9] There is evidence that the labour market is imperfect and characterised by market power in both rural and urban areas (Bardhan and Rudra 1981; Bardhan 1979, 1984; Binswanger et al. 1984; Card and Krueger 1995; Datt 1997; Manning 2005). Mukherji (2005) explored the relationship between wages and employment in a spectrum of labour market structure. He argued that when the labour market is non-competitive, the "unique link" between wages and employment break down, and thus, the rise in minimum wage does not necessarily reduce the employment.

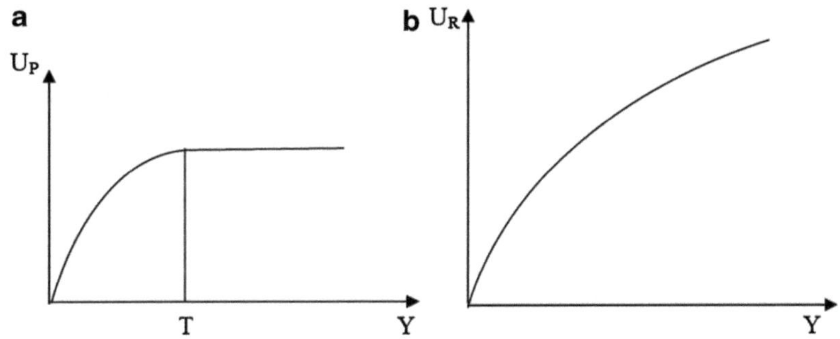

Fig. 7.3 (**a**) Utility function of the poor household. (**b**) Utility function of the rich household

an aspiration income level of the poor household. Another way of stating this is that the utility function from income for the poor is concave up to the income level *T* and then flattens out such that there is no extra utility from any addition to income beyond *T*.[10] Let *y* represent income.

$$\text{Formally,} U_{\text{p}} = u(y) \text{ where } u'(y) > 0 \text{ and } u''(y) < 0 \text{ for } y < T \text{ and } u'(y) = 0 \text{ and } u''(y) = 0 \text{ for } y \geq T$$

For the rich household, utility is always an increasing function of income (Fig. 7.3). So

$$U_{\text{R}} = u(y) \text{ where } u'(y) > 0 \quad \text{and} \quad u''(y) < 0 \quad \text{for all } y$$

The reason behind such a difference in the shape of the utility functions for the two types of household could be due to their relative access to certain goods and services. For rich, the utility function is standard as more income makes them better off. This is due to the fact that rich household has access to banking sector both for credit and parking their savings. Their children would normally go to school, creating opportunities for more income being productively spent. They will have better standard of living with other household accessories where additional income would create additional opportunities for deriving more utility. On the other hand, for the poor the above opportunities are very limited and additional income may not always involve productive spending, leading to higher utility for them. In most cases, their children either do not go to school or go to free government schools. The poor typically also do not save in the bank. Data on household expenditure from the National Sample Survey (NSS) also reveals that the scope for spending on goods and services other than the basic ones is very limited for the rural poor, and hence the marginal

[10] Basu et al. (2010) used a similar utility function for the household in the context of child labour supply. They found that given the fixed target income of the household, the child labour supply behaves as inverted U shape with respect to the landholding of the household.

utility of income after a level will be negligible in the short run. NSS data from 2007 to 2008 reveals that the household expenditure on elastic items (medical, educational, entertainment, toiletries, footwear, consumer services, etc.) is about Rs. 60 per month (15% of total monthly per capita expenditure) (National Sample Survey: NSS Report no. 530).

7.2.3 Absence of NREGA

Now consider the decision problem of the poor household in the above setup without the presence of NREGA programme. Given the labour days available with the family, they would have two options to allocate their total labour. Suppose the prevailing wage rate is w. First, consider the possibility of $w > w^*$: the case of labour surplus economy. In the prevailing wage, there would be excess supply of labour. Each rich household would employ l_s such that $f'(K, L+l_s)=w$. So the total amount of labour demand would be $m.l_s$. Assuming that the total demand for labour is shared equally by all the poor households, each poor household would supply ml_s / n. In such an economy, the poor family would try to reach as close to the income target as possible. Therefore, out of the rest of the labour $(L - ml_s / n)$, the poor household would employ on their own field so far as the marginal productivity of labour is zero. The excess labour remains totally unemployed due to the lack of opportunities.[11]

Next, we move on to the possibility where there is no excess supply of labour at the prevailing wage and the market equilibrium can be obtained such that at a reasonable wage the demand and supply equate. However, the imperfection in the labour market manifests in the form of lower prevailing wage than the equilibrium wage that could be ensured by the free play of demand and supply forces. This is the case of wage suppression mentioned earlier. Thus, we assume that $0 < w < w^*$. Given the prevailing wage, the poor household would employ a part, say l_p, in their own field such that $f'(k, l_p)=w$. The remaining labour supply is $L-l_p$.[12] So there are two possibilities: either they supply the entire surplus labour to rich household or they supply less than the available labour days with them.

Case 1: *Income below the target for the poor*: The poor household supply the entire surplus labour and get $w(L-l_p)$. Their total income is $f(k, l_p)+w(L-l_p)$. They will supply the entire surplus labour to the rich household at the prevailing wage, provided that

$$f(k, l_p) + w(L - l_p) < T \qquad 7.2$$

[11] Here we have presumed that with excess supply of labour it is not possible to reach the target income with such a low wage for the poor households.

[12] Note that if the wage rate $w > w_h$, then the poor would decide not to cultivate their land and only supply the labour to the rich household. In that case $l_p = 0$. This is the case when the poor households become agricultural labourers and stop cultivating their own land.

Case 2: *Income at the target for the poor*: If the opposite happens, that is, $f(k, l_p)+w(L-l_p)>T$, the poor household would not supply the entire surplus labour to the rich household. They will work for say l_s labour days for the rich household such that $f(k, l_p)+wl_s=T$. And as a result $l_p+l_s<L$ (the poor household's endowment of labour).

Note that in Case 1, at the prevailing wage, the entire excess labour days from all poor households is absorbed in the production of rich households, and given that the prevailing wage is below the equilibrium wage w^*, there would be excess demand for labour. The wage does not adjust to equilibrium given the labour market imperfection and the related socioeconomic factors, which keeps the wage lower than the equilibrium wage, though there exist an upward pressure on the wage.

On the other hand, in Case 2 the poor household reaches their target income by their own cultivation and selling a portion of their surplus labour in the market. And given that the household has reached the target income, any increase in wage would bring down the total employment of labour of the poor household (l_p+l_s). Now the supply of labour in response to the increase in wage to the rich household would depend on the sensitivity of the MPL in the poor household's land. Thus, there is a substitution between the employment in own cultivation and market supply to rich household. It is possible that the market supply may be backward bending given that the overall choice of labour supply to own cultivation and market supply is diminishing in response to wage increase. With such a backward-bending supply of labour, it is conceivable that an equilibrium may not exist for small increase in wage and we may have a situation of excess demand for a wide range of wages. This happens due to the scarcity of labour. Another possibility could be the existence of multiple equilibria in the labour market. How far the wage would adjust to bring about an equilibrium in the labour market depends on the degree of imperfection. If the rich household can perfectly collude and set the wage for the labour market, then they would set the wage at a level which maximises the total supply of labour to the rich households, that is, the wage which just allow the poor households to reach their target incomes. This wage may not equal the equilibrating value.

Case 1 is amply illustrated by the perfect labour market analysis in Fig. 7.2. However, for Case 2, Fig. 7.4 would be useful to understand the outcome (Basu et al. (2010) consider a somewhat similar situation in terms of child labour supply). It is clear from the diagram that labour supply would be backward bending and there are possibilities of multiple equilibria in the labour market. It is also possible that even if the wages are allowed to adjust upward, the magnitude of adjustment has to be fairly large. It is also possible that after a large wage adjustment for an equilibrium, the poor household might stop cultivating their own land.[13]

The possible existence of inverse relationship between labour supply and wage for some categories of workers in developing countries was subject to scrutiny by various authors. Traditionally, the study of backward-bending supply curve was

[13] There is also the possibility that the poor households reach their target income only from cultivating their own land. In that case the labour market vanishes at the prevailing wage. We leave this uninteresting case out.

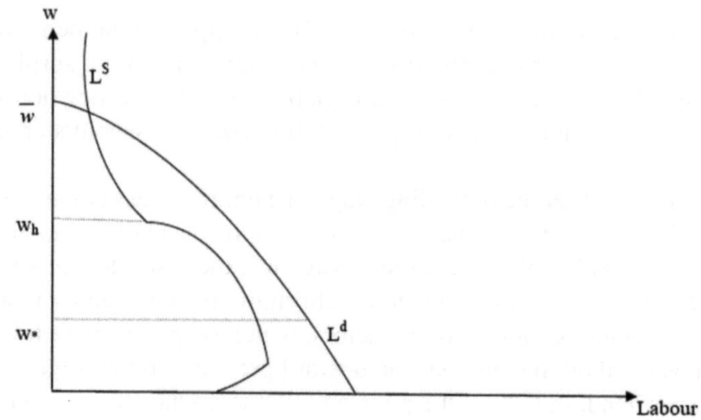

Fig. 7.4 The labour supply from the poor households when their earnings are on target

based on the assumptions of "target income" (Berg 1961), "limited aspiration" (Mellor 1963) and "subsistence mentality" (Lewis 1954). An early study by Berg (1961) posed the problem in terms of "target income" for the migrant labour in a dual economy structure and argued that "the aggregate labor supply function to any given country (say the Union of South Africa, or the Ivory Coast or Uganda) may have been backward-sloping in the early years of African development". Among some of the recent studies, the studies by Licona (2000) for Mexico, Dessing (2002) for Philippines, Bhalotra (2007) for child labour in Pakistan, El-Hamidi (2003) for female labour in Egypt and Sharif (1991) for Bangaldesh are noteworthy. In Indian context, Bardhan (1979) mentioned that "there seems to be some evidence for at least a locally back-ward-bending supply curve of labor for the set of all adult women (primarily house-wives) and of hired-out farm labor for the set of cultivators of all size groups taken together" in his sample of 8,500 rural workers from nearly 4,900 households drawn from about 500 sample villages belonging to the state of West Bengal. Lately, Dasgupta and Goldar (2005) investigated the issue for rural female labour supply using NSS data for 1999–2000, and they found that "supply of female labour from below poverty line households in rural areas is inversely related to wage rate and the number of earning members in the family", and thus, as early as 2005, they raised doubt about the efficacy of National Rural Employment Guarantee Scheme.

7.2.4 Impact of NREGA

Under NREGA, a certain number of days of labour employment are provided by the government scheme. Assume that number to be *x*. In this section, we consider the case where the NREGA work is just an employment scheme and no assets are created which influence the productivity of land. As a result, the production functions for rich and poor households remain as they were before.

It is an empirical fact that the NREGA wage is higher than the prevailing wage rate in most areas (see Table 7.2, columns 5 and 6, a notable exception being the state of Gujarat). For a poor household, there are three options to work and try to reach the target income. Assume the NREGA wage is $w^N > w$, which is the prevailing wage.

7.2.4.1 Case of Labour Surplus Economy

In case of the labour surplus economy, the impact of NREGA depends on the relative magnitude of NREGA work and the amount of surplus labour in the economy. If the amount of NREGA work is below the surplus labour available in each poor household, then there would be no impact of NREGA work on the employment decision for their own cultivation and the decision to supply labour for the rich households. As a result of NREGA work, the level of outputs in both rich and poor households remains the same, but the NREGA work would increase the income of the poor households. This prediction is based on the presumption that that NREGA work of 100 labour days does not still allow the poor households to reach their target level of income (but it is still comparatively substantial as illustrated in Table 7.2, last 4 columns. Here it is seen that, assuming a household of size 5, the earnings from NREGA alone is sufficient to cover 30–50% of the income required to be above the poverty line. The percentage is closer to 60% assuming households with four members.). If the amount of NREGA works available is more than the surplus labour available in each poor household, then there would be some change in the employment decision of the poor households and the analysis is similar to what is given below for any economy with or without surplus labour. This additional demand from NREGA work would reduce the supply of labour to the rich households.

The poor households try to maximise $y = f(k, l_p) + w^N.x + wl_s \leq T$ subject to $l_p + x + l_s \leq L$.

Possibility 1: If $y = f(k, l_p(w^N)) + w^N.x \geq T$, then the poor households would not even undertake the full amount of NREGA work allotted to them. So they may not even work for x labour days and would choose the amount of work $z \leq x$ such that $y = f(k, l_p(w^N)) + w^N.z = T$. In this scenario, the labour market would vanish. As compared to the regime without NREGA, it is clear that the agricultural production in poor households would be less, and also the production in the rich household would be less, leading to an overall adverse production effect. Though the presence of NREGA improves the lot of the poor but due to the labour shortage (in this case the labour supply for the rich household vanishes completely), the rich households would be worse off.

Possibility 2: If $y = f(k, l_p(w)) + w^N.x \geq T > f(k, l_p(w^N)) + w^N.x$. The poor household would choose l for its own cultivation such that $l < l_p(w)$ and $y = f(k, l_p(w)) + w^N.x = T$. So they would not supply any labour to the rich household but only employ the labour for self-cultivation and do the full amount of NREGA work and hence reach their target income. Here also the labour market vanishes altogether.

Possibility 3: When $y = f(k, l_p(w)) + w^N.x < T$, the poor would still like to supply some labour to the rich households at the prevailing wage w. Now the poor household would supply (1) the entire surplus labour $L - l_p(w)) - x$ if $y = f(k, l_p(w^N)) + w^N.x + w$

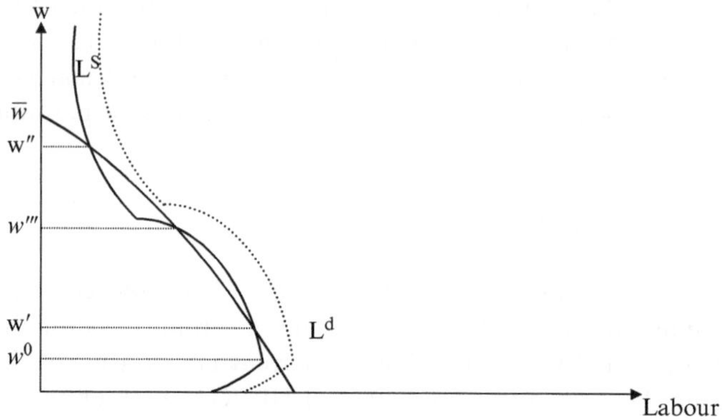

Fig. 7.5 Possibility of multiple equilibria post NREGA

$(L - l_P(w^N)) - x) < T$ or (2) supply $l_N < (L - l_P(w^N)) - x$ such that $y = f(k,\ l_P(w^N)) + w^N.x + wl_N = T$.

Thus, we have three possible outcomes of the economy with the introduction of the NREGA scheme. There is no supply to the labour market and the target income of the poor is reached by their own cultivation and NREGA work (Possibilities 1 and 2). In Possibility 3, the labour market exists and the target of the poor may or may not be reached.

It is obvious that, in the presence of NREGA, starting from the same situation, a poor household would supply less labour to the market than could be hired by the rich household. As a result, there will be adverse production effect, and the poor household would be better off, but the rich households would be worse off. Note that with the introduction of NREGA, given that the NREGA wage is higher than the prevailing market wage, the poor household would always prefer to work for the NREGA scheme. The market supply is only related to how the remaining labour days are being allocated between own cultivation and the market supply.

Remark: When the target of the poor households is fulfilled with only partial supply of their labour to the market, then any attempt to increase the wage in the market for bringing more labour supply to the market may be counterproductive as the labour supply to the market would eventually be backward bending with large increase in the market wage w (Possibility 3). On the other hand, when the target of the poor household is not reached even with supply of labour to the market, then with the increase in wage it is possible to bring forth more labour to the market (Fig. 7.5).

The above figure shows the possibility of multiple equilibria after the NREGA scheme is implemented starting from an initial situation where there was only one equilibrium. There are three equilibria: two of them are stable and the middle one is unstable. If the market plays itself out perfectly, then the equilibrium wages are all above the initial one. However, given the labour supply curve, if the rich households can organise themselves and cooperate, they would fix the wage at w^0, which would maximise the total labour supply to the rich households.

7.3 NREGA: Productivity Link

The above observations are made with the assumption that NREGA work does not affect the production function of the agricultural sector at all. Since NREGA works are to create some social assets which would have impact on the productivity of the agriculture by facilitating irrigation and water conservation, roads and rural marketing, etc., we now introduce that NREGA work improves the productivity in agriculture by a factor ε. Thus, the production function becomes $Q=(1+\varepsilon)\,f(\cdot)$ for both type of households. Given the public good nature of the asset creation to enhance productivity in agriculture, we assume that the productivity increases symmetrically for both rich and poor households.

Now due to this productivity increase in the land, the marginal productivity of labour shifts outwards for both households with fixed amount of land. Thus, for any prevailing wage, the poor would like to employ more labour in their own land, leaving less available for NREGA work or for the labour market. This rise in productivity increases the likelihood that the poor reaches their target income easily. Thus, the rise in productivity increases the chance either that the labour market vanishes or the poor household reaches their target income without supplying the whole surplus labour to the labour market.

First, we consider the case of labour surplus economy. Suppose, the NREGA work is just sufficient to absorb the surplus labour from the economy. Given that labourers are fully employed, there would be upward pressure on the wage to bring about more labour for the cultivation of rich household. Even if the wage increases in response to NREGA work or even if the level of employment in both rich and poor household remains the same absent NREGA work, production in both households increases and both the rich and poor households are better off. This situation can only arise if the poor households do not reach their target income even after the NREGA works provided to them. In case the poor reaches the target income and there is less or no supply of labour to the rich household, this would be a negative factor despite the increase in productivity. The overall effect on the level of production can go in either direction.

Now we consider the situation where there exists a labour market in the absence of NREGA and the poor household does not reach their target income due to the low wage in the economy.

Considering the worst possible scenario in the absence of NREGA, the poor households could not reach their target income even though they supply the surplus labour entirely to the market. Now with the introduction of NREGA, the productivity of the land increases. This results into more labour to be employed in the land of poor household. Now even after undertaking the NREGA work, there may or may not be surplus labour for the market. Consider the extreme form of productivity increase which is very high so that there is no surplus labour for the market and the poor households target incomes are reached. The labour market vanishes altogether. The poors are necessarily better off. The rich household would also be better off for very high productivity increase if the following condition is satisfied:

$$(1+\varepsilon)f(K,L) > f\left(K, L+\frac{ml_s}{n}\right)$$

It is not so clear from the above expression what happens for a relatively small or moderate productivity increase. It would depend on the relative change in labour supply vis-à-vis the relative change in productivity, and the effect can go either way. In general, one can expect that if the NREGA leads to a relatively small productivity increase compared to a relatively large drop in the labour supply the overall production will go down, whereas if there is relatively large productivity increase and relatively little change in labour supply in response to NREGA, there would be positive output effect.

7.3.1 *Numerical Example*

The following numerical example illustrates an interesting possibility where the output effect would be non-monotonic in relation to increase in productivity.

Consider a village with one rich household and three poor households.[14] The rich household has a land holding of 625 units and each of the poor household has 4 units of land. The wage in the market is $w=60$ and each household has the amount of labour available $L=200$. The poor household has a target income $T=12{,}000$. The NREGA wage $w^N=100$ and the total amount of NREGA work available per household $x=40$ labour days.

The agricultural production function: land (k) and labour (l)

$$Q = (1+\varepsilon)\left\{100\sqrt{kl} - 2l^2\right\}$$

Given the production function, the marginal productivity of labour is given by

$$\frac{\partial Q}{\partial l} = (1+\varepsilon)\left\{100\sqrt{k} - 4l\right\}$$

Thus, the marginal productivity of labour is a linear function and attains zero at the level of employment $l=25\sqrt{k}$. The marginal productivity of labour for rich household is

$$(1+\varepsilon)(2{,}500-4l).$$

[14] One can increase the size of the village by replicating the number of households in the given proportion, and all our results in this section would still hold true.

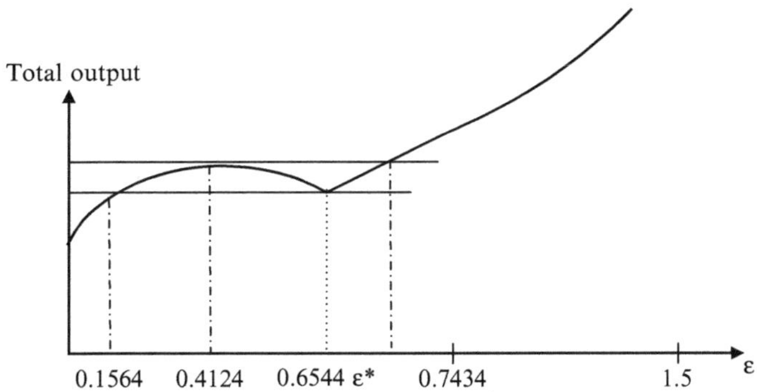

Fig. 7.6 Total production for the example where $\varepsilon^* = .736$ (approximately).

Similarly, for the poor households: $(1+\varepsilon)(200-4l)$.

Note that this production function obeys the diminishing marginal productivity property for land as well. However, in case of land the marginal productivity curve is convex.

Routine calculation would show that for different ranges of productivity parameter we can plot the behaviour of the total output of the economy as below (Fig. 7.6).[15]

The figure shows that there exists a non-monotonic relationship between the increase in productivity and the total output produced in both poor and rich households together. For an initial range, the poor household still supplies labour to the rich household, but this is decreasing. These two effects balances at a point $\varepsilon = .4124$ and then the output starts falling up to $\varepsilon = .6544$. After that, the labour market vanishes for the rich household and subsequent increase in productivity increases the total output in the economy. This is a very interesting result as the programme like NREGA despite having the strong productivity enhancement effect (up to 65%) can still lead to decrease in total output in the economy.

The output starts falling when the increase in productivity is beyond .4124 and up to .6544. However, the output increases as productivity increases up to 1.5 at which the labour supply even for the NREGA work goes to zero. The labour supply to NREGA work comes to a halt at $\varepsilon = 1.5$, and so without the labour supply for NREGA, the productivity increase cannot take place. The purpose of this example is illustrative and it is not conceivable that such a drastic productivity increase would at all take place from the NREGA scheme itself.

We have checked in the above example the behaviour of total output when there are one rich and only one poor households in the economy. Then the increase in productivity always leads to an increase in the total output in the economy. Keeping in view that the annual increase in productivity of the agriculture in India is around 3%, in the above example we have tried with another set of parameter configurations.

[15] The detailed calculation can be obtained from the authors on request.

Using the same set of production functions for the rich and poor farmers with the days of NREGA works increased to 60 days and the number of poor farmers increased to six households, we have found that with respect to productivity increase the total agricultural production goes up until 2% increase in productivity and then starts falling until 27% productivity increase and then again starts increasing from there onwards for all values of productivity growth. Thus, we also demonstrate that the relative distribution of the rich and poor households in the economy is extremely important for understanding the effect of productivity increase on the overall output in agriculture as a result of NREGA scheme.

7.4 Empirical Support

It is too early to assess the impact of NREGA with respect to the broad parameters of our framework that we have developed in our theoretical section. Although there is government data with respect to the coverage, spending, number of work days created, people participation, etc., in the NREGA programmes since its inception, however, there is no attempt by the researchers to undertake rigorous empirical work to pin down the possible effects and interlinkages with other activities in the economy. The focus of the existing empirical studies, which are few in number, is to analyse the success or failures of this scheme in different areas and how the scheme has benefitted the people who participated in it. There are considerable concerns about the implementation of the scheme in certain areas and the leakages that arise due to corrupt practices. However, whatever little empirical case studies are available, they have glossed over the fundamental issues that are raised in this chapter such as the impact on the labour market in terms of demand and supply, and wages and the impact on the overall agricultural production or other activities such as self-employment. These are important parameters for evaluating a programme like NREGA, and we hope that researchers would pay attention to these parameters while undertaking empirical studies in the future. Below we report some of the empirical studies which validate our concern to some extent. These studies are indicative and not conclusive given their obvious limitations in the methodology.

7.4.1 NREGA: Demand for Employment

Nair et al. (2009) studied the impact of the National Rural Employment Guarantee Programme in three Grama Panchayats of Kasaragod District of Kerala, namely, Madikai, Ajanoor and Trikarpur. While the worker registration is appreciably good in all the three Grama Panchayats including registration of SC and ST categories, however, there is a sharp drop in the number of people who demanded jobs in 2007–2008 which was below one-fourth in two Panchayats and just above one-third in the third Panchayat. There was further drop in the number in the following year.

The relationship of the NREGA wage rate with the state minimum wage rate has also been a complex and contentious issue. Initially the NREGA wage rate was linked to the state minimum wage and consequently helped to push up the minimum wage in the laggard states. But this increased the burden on the central exchequer. Finally, in 2009, the NREGA wage rate was delinked from the state minimum, and immediately several rights group started criticising this move fearing "Minimum wages began to be enforced only after NREGS was pegged to it… delinking will again reduce the Minimum Wage Act to a well-meaning, but poorly enforced law" (*The Economic Times*, 5 April 2011).[16]

In fact it is now in public debate also whether the NREGA scheme has been a social failure by substituting labour away from productive usage, which only added to the burden of the exchequer. It is a matter which is being actively discussed in the media and the policy circles with the government reconsidering the parameters that drive this policy. A recent study by CRISIL (Mahambare and Nadkarni 2011) using NSS data reports that between the years 2004–2005 and 2009–2010 self-employment in agriculture has shrunk by 25.5 million (National Sample Survey: NSS Report no. 509). They conclude that one of the major contributing factors could be the increased dependence on the government's social security safety net, "…while NREGA improved wages and incomes in rural areas, it appears to have prompted more people to drop out of self-employment and increased dependency on the state dole".

There are cases of conflict between NREGA work and agricultural work in the peak seasons, leading to reduced supply of labour for the agricultural activity. The NREGA works in states like Uttar Pradesh and Bihar have also reduced the supply of migrant labourers to Punjab and Haryana and other places. Since the time NREGA came into force, the cost of agriculture labour has gone up in many parts of the country quite substantially, and given the low productivity of some of the agricultural activities, it is also true that farming is becoming unviable with the increase in labour costs in many areas. In view of such outcomes, recently, the Ministry of Agriculture has specifically asked the Ministry of Rural Development to stop the NREGA works in some peak agricultural seasons of sowing, transplantation and harvesting (The Hindustan Times, 14 July 2011). It is apparent that a major overhaul in the scheme is forthcoming soon (*The Economic Times*, 1 August 2011).

7.4.2 NREGA: Productivity

With the adverse production effect and increase in the income of the poor households who spend most part of their income on food and other essential items, the introduction of NREGA would necessarily lead to rise in food prices unless the food

---

[16] Nikhil Dey, the Mazdoor Kisan Shakti Sangathan.

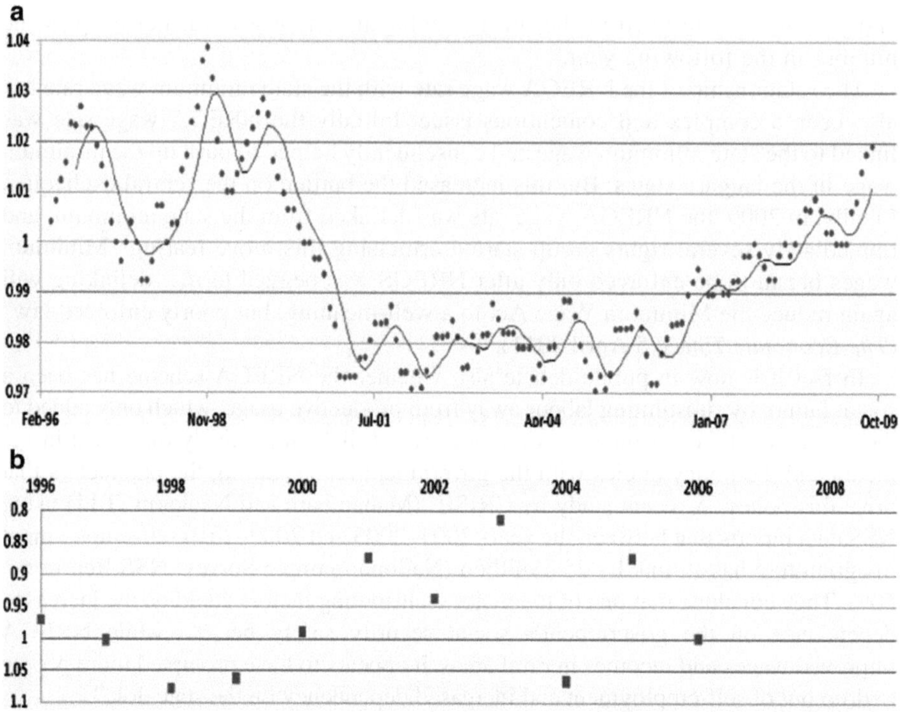

Fig. 7.7 (**a**) Food price to overall ratio for CPI, Agricultural Labourers (April 1996 to September 2009). (**b**) Ratio of actual to normal annual rainfall, 1995–2006

prices are stabilised with imports. Whether imports are a viable option for long term from the world market is another debate which we do not want to go into in this chapter. To verify the price rise possibility, we look at the relative price of food items with respect to the CPI (consumer price index), particularly for the agricultural labourers (see Fig. 7.7a). The data spans the period February 1996 to October 2009. The overall pattern does not reveal any specific trend with a high relative food price zone in the late 1990s followed by a cheaper phase in the early 2000s but which shows a gradual upward movement in the last 4 years. Thus, it is apparent that there has been a sharp rise in the relative price of food items since the inception of NREGA in 2005. This has happened in a period with no change in government and no big climatic events.

To check whether this has been due to a poor rainfall and hence overall decrease in agricultural production, in Fig. 7.7b, we have also presented the rainfall deficit by plotting the actual rainfall as a percentage of "ideal" rainfall levels (according to meteorological standards). Although this data only covers up to 2006, what we can see is that the rainfall in 2004 and 2006 has not been below average with one slightly bad year in between. In fact, on average the rainfall situation has been better in the period 2004–2006 compared to the previous 9 years. But during the later period, the relative price has taken a sharp and monotone upward move. Thus, we can detect no clear linkage between the rise in food price and annual rainfall levels. This further strengthens our intuition of a possible linkage between the policy inception and the price rise.

7.5 Concluding Remarks

A crucial dimension of the rural labour market is the target income of the poor. This target income is the root cause of the backward-bending supply curve of labour in our analysis. So the policy focus should be to increase this target income by creating more market access and opportunities for the poor households and improving their standard of living. In other words, in the current scenario with limited opportunities for productive spending and market access, it is unlikely that just generating extra income would alone solve the problem. Consider a poor household who wants to buy a TV set or other electronic equipments which would improve their quality of living. But without electricity connection or with extremely irregular supply of electricity to rural areas, it is impossible for a poor household to enjoy the benefit properly. As a result, the household may prefer to live without such household accessories which otherwise would have improved the quality of their living. The similar problem of market access arises when it comes to educating their children. Even though the poor household is interested in good education of their children, there may not be any good school in the neighbourhood. The poor households in most cases avoid banking sector for parking their savings as the process of dealing with a bank requires some level of education which most poor households do not have. Thus, to enhance the opportunities for the poor, the policy should be inclusive and multipronged. Thus, the target income may be enhanced by creating opportunities and market access from multiple dimensions and not just an income generating scheme like NREGA can help to improve the situation of the poor households.

In order to avoid the adverse production effect arising out of reduction of labour supply from the poor households, we need a direct policy of agricultural productivity increase such as another green revolution along with mechanisation so that a large part of agricultural activity can be done by machine which will replace the labour in agriculture. It is also important to revisit patterns of land holdings in states like West Bengal where the successful land reform has created too much fragmentation and such tiny plots of land are a deterrent for large scale mechanisation of agriculture. So, we also suggest a consolidation of land holdings wherever necessary.

Most of our results are tentative predictions from a simple conceptual framework involving the NREGA scheme. Future researchers must investigate the truth of some of the predictions empirically. Our testable hypotheses are:

1. Wages have gone up in response to NREGA scheme.
2. Do people refuse to work even at higher wage in peak agricultural seasons (during sowing or harvesting seasons) while they have worked for NREGA in lean seasons?

3. There has been improvement in agricultural productivity due to NREGA.
4. There has been a net loss in agricultural production in sync with the implementation of NREGA.

Given the significant impact of NREGA scheme in the rural labour market as we have depicted in this chapter, it is possible to have a reverse migration from urban to rural areas. That is, we may observe a Lewis model in reverse, urban industrial workers coming back to agricultural area in search of easy NREGA wage. Though there is casual empirical evidence on this, however, no proper empirical study is available on this aspect of NREGA.

Acknowledgement We are grateful to Nancy Chau, Deepti Goel, Bishwantath Goldar and J. V. Meenakshi for helpful comments on an earlier version of this chapter.

References

Bardhan P (1979) Labor supply functions in a poor agrarian economy. Am Econ Rev 69:73–83

Bardhan P (1984) Land, labor, and rural poverty: essays in development economics. Oxford University Press, Delhi

Bardhan PK, Rudra A (1981) Terms and conditions of labour contracts in agriculture: results of a survey in West Bengal 1979. Oxford Bulletin of Economics and Statistics 43, 1 February. Bernstein, Irving, 1970. Turbulent years: a history of the American Worker, 1933–1941. Houghton Mifflin, Boston

Basu K (1981) Food for work programmes: beyond roads that get washed away. Economic and Political Weekly, 3–10 January

Basu K (1997) Analytical development economics: the less developed economy revisited. MIT Press, Cambridge

Basu AK (2007) Impact of rural employment guarantee schemes on seasonal labor markets: optimum compensation and workers' welfare. College of William and Mary, Mimeo

Basu A, Chau N, Ravi K (2005) The National Rural Employment Guarantee Act of India, Entry for the Oxford Companion to Economics in India

Basu K, Das S, Dutta B (2010) Child labor and household wealth: theory and empirical evidence of an inverted-U. J Develop Econ 91:8–14

Berg E (1961) Backward-sloping labor supply function in dual economies – African ease. Q J Econ 75(3):468–492

Bernstein I (1970) Turbulent Years: a history of the American Worker, 1933–1941. Houghton Mifflin, Boston

Besley T, Coate S (1992) Workfare vs. welfare: incentive arguments for work requirements in poverty alleviation programs. Am Econ Rev 82(2):249–261

Besley T, Kanbur R (1993) Principles of targeting. In: Lipton M, van de Gaag J (eds) Including the poor: proceedings of a symposium organized by The World Bank and The International Food Policy Research Institute. The World Bank, Washington, DC, pp 67–90

Bhalla SS (2004) Ten Lies and an Act: I. Business Standard, 25 Dec 2004

Bhalotra S (2007) Is child work necessary? Oxford Bull Econ Stat 69(1):29–55

Binswanger HP, Doherty VS, Balaramaiah T, Bhende MJ, Kshirsagar KG, Rao VB, Raju PSS (1984) Common features and contrasts in labor relations in the semiarid tropics of India. In: Binswanger H, Rosenzweig M (eds) Contractual arrangements, employments, and wages in rural labor markets in Asia. Yale University Press, New Haven, pp 143–168

Blaug M (1963) The myth of the old poor law and the making of the new. J Econ Hist 23:151–184
Blaug M (1964) The poor law report re-examined. J Econ Hist 24:229–245
Card D, Krueger AB (1995) Myth and measurement: the new economics of the minimum wage. Princeton University Press, Princeton
Dasgupta P, Goldar B (2005) Female labour supply in rural India: an econometric analysis. Discussion Paper, E/265/2005. Institute of Economic Growth, Delhi
Datt G (1997) Bargaining power, wages and employment: an analysis of agricultural labor markets in India. Sage, London
Dessing M (2002) Labour supply, the family and poverty: the S-shaped labour supply curve. J Econ Behav Organ 49:433–458
Drèze J, Khera R (2009) The battle for employment guarantee. Frontline 26(01), 3–16
Drèze J, Sen A (1991) Strategies of entitlement protection. Chapter 7, In Hunger and public action, Oxford University Press, pp 104–121
El-Hamidi F (2003) Poverty and labour supply of women: evidence from Egypt. Paper presented at tenth annual conference of the Economic Research Forum, 16–18 December
Kesselman JR (1978) Work relief programs in the great depression. In: Palmer JL (ed) Creating jobs: public employment programs and wage subsidies. Brookings Institution, Washington, DC
Lewis WA (1954) Economic development with unlimited supplies of labor. Manch Sch Econ Soc Stud 22:139–91
Licona GH (2000) Reshaping the labour supply curve for the poor. Paper presented at the annual meeting of the Latin American and Caribbean Economic Association, Rio
Lipton M (1996) Success in anti-poverty. Issues in development discussion paper, vol 8. International Labour Office, Geneva
Mahambare V, Nadkarni R (2011) Unemployment in India: uneven and weak. A study by CRISIL Centre for Economic Research, CRISIL Research Report Employment Eco Insight, India
Manning A (2005) Monopsony in motion: imperfect competition in labor markets. Princeton University Press, Princeton
Mathur L (2007) Employment guarantee: progress so far. Economic & Political Weekly, 29 Dec 2007
Mehrotra S (2008) NREG two years on: where do we go from here? Economic & Political Weekly, 2 Aug
Mellor JW (1963) The use and productivity of farm family labor in early stages of agricultural development. J Farm Econ 45(3), 517–534
Mukherji A (2005) On wages and employment. Ind J Lab Econ 49:66–77
Nair KN, Sreedharan TP, Anoopkumar M (2009) A study of National Rural Employment Guarantee Programme in three grama panchayats of Kasaragod district, Working paper 413, Centre for Development Studies, Trivandrum, India
National Sample Survey: NSS Report no. 509. Household consumption of various goods and services in India, 2004–2005, NSS 61st Round, July 2004–June 2005
National Sample Survey: NSS Report no. 530. Household consumer expenditure in India, 2007–08, NSS 64th Round, July 2007–June 2008
Ravallion M (1990) Market responses to anti-hunger policies: effects on wages prices and employment. In: Drèze J, Sen A (eds) The political economy of hunger. Clarendon, Oxford
Ravallion M (1991) Reaching the rural poor through EGS employment: arguments, lessons, and evidence from South Asia. World Bank Res Obs 6(1):153–176
Ravallion M, Datt G, Chaudhuri S (1993) Does Maharashtra's employment guarantee scheme guarantee employment? Effects of the 1988 wage increase. Econ Dev Cult Chang 41(2):251–275
Ray D (1998) Development economics. Princeton University Press, Princeton
Rajshekhar M. Can Centre fix NREGS wages in isolation? The Economic Times, 5 Apr 2011 http://www.im4change.org/rural-news-update/can-centre-fix-nregs-wages-in-isolation-by-m-rajshekhar-6961.html
Banerji D. UPA Govt's NREGA back on table for removing flaws, The Economic Times, 1 Aug 2011 http://articles.economictimes.indiatimes.com/2011-08-01/news/29838758_1_rural-roads-scheme-national-rural-employment-guarantee

Ghose S. The idiocy of urban thinking, The Hindustan Times, 14 Feb 2008 http://www.hindustantimes.com/editorial-views-on/Platform/The-idiocy-of-urban-thinking/Article1-275862.aspx
Prasad N. Ministry seeks to halt job plan in farm season, The Hindustan Times, 14 July 2011 http://www.hindustantimes.com/India-news/NewDelhi/Ministry-seeks-to-halt-job-plan-in-farm-season/Article1-721231.aspx
Von Braun J (1995) Employment for poverty reduction and food security. International Food Policy Research Institute, Washington, DC

Web References

http://www.agricoop.nic.in/
http://nrega.nic.in/netnrega/home.aspx

Chapter 8
Measuring Efficiency of Technical Education Institutions in Kerala Using Data Envelopment Analysis

S. Sunitha and Malathy Duraisamy

8.1 Introduction

India has the third largest higher education system (next to USA and China) and the second largest stock of scientific and technical manpower in the world. The higher educational system in India has witnessed remarkable developments such as near-stagnant or declining trend in government spending on the sector, increasing gross enrolment ratio (GER) and entry of private players (domestic and foreign), amongst other things. India, like many other developing countries, is finding it hard to cope with the increasing financial requirements of an expanding educational system.

In India, education is largely the responsibility of the respective state governments. Therefore, there exist wide disparities in educational achievement across the states. This chapter focuses on higher technical education institutions in Kerala, a southern state in India. Kerala's commendable achievement in human development – literacy, elementary school enrolment and health – is well known. But the progress of higher education in the state has not kept pace with its performance in secondary education (Tilak 2001).

Technical education is an important component of the higher education system, and it comprises engineering, technology, management, architecture, etc. at diploma, degree, postgraduate and research levels. Amongst these disciplines, engineering is

S. Sunitha (✉)
School of Management Studies, National Institute of Technology (NIT) Calicut, Calicut 673601, India
e-mail: sunita@nitc.ac.in

M. Duraisamy
Department of Humanities and Social Sciences, Indian Institute of Technology (IIT) Madras, Chennai 600036, India
e-mail: mdurai@iitm.ac.in

N.S. Siddharthan and K. Narayanan (eds.), *Human Capital and Development: The Indian Experience*, DOI 10.1007/978-81-322-0857-0_8, © Springer India 2013

the dominant one. Interestingly, in Kerala, an increasing role of private sector is observed especially in engineering (degree) education where about 85% of institutions are self-financing institutions. The government however continues to play a major role in technical education (diploma) imparted through the polytechnic institutions.

Given the role of the government in technical education in Kerala and the public resources allocated to this sector, it is important to evaluate the resource use efficiency of these institutions. Further, in the light of the increasing role of private sector (private-aided, government-owned self-supported and private-unaided or self-financing institutions) in the recent period, it would be useful to assess and compare the efficiency across different types of institutions. This chapter makes an attempt in this direction by using a non-parametric approach, namely, data envelopment analysis (DEA). To our knowledge, attempts to measure efficiency of higher education institutions are rather scanty, particularly based on DEA methodology.

The remainder of the chapter is organised as follows: Sect. 8.2 presents a discussion on the concepts of and methods to evaluate efficiency in higher education. Section 8.3 provides a brief discussion on DEA approach. This is followed by a brief survey of recent literature and outline of the data and specification of inputs and outputs. Focus is then placed on the definition of alternative specifications of performance in higher education, with reports on empirical results from the application of our methodology on higher technical education institutions in Kerala. Finally, the policy implications and conclusions of our research are discussed.

8.2 Efficiency of Higher Education Institutions (HEIs)

The three major measures that are often evaluated in the context of HEIs are technical, allocative and scale efficiency, respectively. Intuitively, technical efficiency is a measure of the extent to which an institution efficiently allocates the physical inputs at its disposal for a given level of output. The first step in determining efficiency is to identify some standard or benchmark from which estimates can be derived. This is done by identifying those institutions using the least amount of inputs per output. By fitting a line through these observations, one creates an envelope or frontier from which the inefficiency in other institutions can be evaluated. Thus, technical efficiency captures the extent to which physical inputs are efficiently allocated. The second efficiency measure is allocative[1] or price efficiency which measures the extent to which inefficiency occurs because an institution is using the 'wrong' combination of inputs given what they cost to purchase. A third type of efficiency is economic or overall efficiency which jointly considers technical and allocative efficiencies. Finally, a frequently estimated measure in respect of higher education institutions is scale efficiency. Many

[1] The dearth of data on input prices makes it difficult to estimate allocative efficiency.

empirical studies on higher education costs seek to measure the extent to which institutions are operating at increasing (decreasing) returns to scale, which in turn helps to determine the optimal size of an institution.

There are two basic approaches to estimate a production function: the statistical (or econometric) approach and the nonstatistical (or programming) approach. The statistical approach is often parametric where one specifies an explicit functional form for the frontier and econometrically estimates the parameters using sample data for inputs and output, and, hence, the accuracy of the derived technical efficiency estimates is sensitive to the nature of the functional form specified. In addition, this method cannot be easily applied to situations involving multiple inputs and multiple outputs, an important characteristic of higher education.

In contrast, the method of data envelopment analysis (DEA) introduced by Charnes, Cooper and Rhodes (CCR) (1978) and further generalised by Banker, Charnes and Cooper (BCC) (1984) offers a non-parametric alternative to parametric frontier production function analysis. The multiple-input, multiple-output nature of production in higher education combined with the absence of prices (of both inputs and outputs) makes DEA an attractive choice of methodology in this context, despite its shortcomings. A number of studies have estimated technical and cost efficiency of universities using data envelopment analysis (DEA) as well as the stochastic frontier (SFA) methodology (see Salerno (2003) and Worthington (2001) for a survey).

The present study makes use of DEA to measure the technical and scale efficiency of higher technical education institutions in Kerala. A brief discussion on DEA methodology follows.

8.3 Data Envelopment Analysis

DEA, initiated by Charnes et al. (1978) and building on Farell's (1957) work, is a non-parametric linear programming technique for measuring the relative efficiency of decision-making units (DMUs) that perform the same type of functions and have identical goals and objectives. The method utilises linear programming to 'envelop' observed data and then calculate efficiency based on the distance a unit is from the relatively efficient frontier (the envelope). While several factors have driven widespread adoption of this method, its most appealing feature is the ability to estimate efficiency in complex multi-input/multi-output firms where the underlying production process is not well understood and there is no preconceived functional form imposed on the data in determining the efficient units. That is, DEA estimates the production function of efficient DMUs using piecewise linear programming on the sample data instead of making restrictive assumptions about the underlying production technology. The mathematical programming formulation then accords the evaluated DMU the most favourable weighting of inputs and outputs that the constraints allow. Note that those DMUs indicated as efficient are only efficient in relation to others in the sample.

DEA is a multifactor productivity analysis model for measuring the relative efficiencies of a homogenous set of decision-making units (DMUs). The efficiency score in the presence of multiple input and output factors is defined as the ratio of weighted sum of outputs to weighted sum of inputs.

Assuming that there are n DMUs, each with m inputs and s outputs, the relative efficiency score of a test DMU p is obtained by solving the following model proposed by Charnes et al. (1978):

$$\max \sum_{k=1}^{s} v_k y_{kp} \div \sum_{j=1}^{m} u_j x_{jp}$$

Subject to

$$\sum_{k=1}^{s} v_k y_{ki} \div \sum_{j=i}^{m} u_j x_{ji} v_k, \quad u_j \geq 0 \ \forall k, j \tag{8.10}$$

where

i (indicates DMU) = 1 to n
y_{ki} = amount of output k produced by DMU i, $k = n$ 1 to s
x_{ji} = amount of input j utilised by DMU i, $j = 1$ to m
v_k = weight given to output k
u_j = weight given to input j

The fractional program shown in (8.1) can be converted to a linear program as shown in (8.2). For more details on model development, see Charnes et al. (1978):

$$\max \sum_{k=1}^{s} v^k y_{kp}$$

Subject to

$$\sum_{j=1}^{m} u_j x_{jp} = 1$$

$$\sum_{k=1}^{s} v_k y_{ki} \div \sum_{j=i}^{m} u_j x_{ji} \leq 0 \quad \forall i$$

$$v_k, u_j \geq 0 \quad v_k, j \tag{8.2}$$

The above problem is run n times in identifying the relative efficiency scores of all the DMUs. Each DMU selects input and output weights that maximise its efficiency score. In general, a DMU is considered to be efficient, if it obtains a score of 1 and a score of less than 1 implies that it is inefficient.

The advantages of this method are, first, that there is no need to make behavioural assumptions about the firms, such as cost minimisation or profit maximisation (which would be regarded as inappropriate in the higher education context) and, second, knowledge of input and output prices, which are often unknown in the higher education context, is not required. The lack of assumptions in DEA regarding statistical distributions, however, means that there are no estimates or significance tests of the parameters of the production function, a potentially serious problem if results are sensitive to the specification of inputs and outputs. The analyst is therefore faced with an array of methods for estimating the higher education production function and deriving measures of efficiency.

Efficiency scores from DEA analysis are known to be highly sensitive to both the choice of input and output measures and the inclusion or exclusion of key variables. A serious drawback of DEA is that it does not provide tests of significance of the input or output variables included in the model.

DEA has proven to be a valuable tool for strategic, policy-related and operational problems, particularly in the service and nonprofit sectors. For the typical profit-maximising firm, it is possible to put money values on the inputs of the production process and, in turn, assess its efficiency. Therefore, in a firm, maximum efficiency is achieved when the price of the resources used to make the commodity is equal to the marginal cost of producing it. In education, this is not feasible since many of the outputs are not quantifiable in terms of market prices. The recent studies on efficiency of higher education have relied more on the application of DEA to estimate efficiency. The advantages of DEA have motivated to use this method in evaluating efficiency of HEIs.

Before applying this method to the present study, selected studies that have used the DEA approach to measure efficiency of HEIs are briefly reviewed.

8.3.1 Efficiency of Higher Education Using DEA: Recent Empirical Evidence

Most of the studies in literature on efficiency of HEIs are with respect to the UK. Athanassapoulos and Shale (1997) found that a subset of 6 out of 45 institutions showed satisfactory performance across alternative efficiency tests examined in the UK using DEA approach. Johnes and Johnes (2005) studied costs and efficiency of higher education in UK during the time period of 2000–2001 to 2002–2003. The results show that cost in science is three times higher than arts stream and the efficiency score is comparatively lower in small and more specialised institutions. Johnes (2006) studied the technical efficiency of higher education institutions (HEIs) in England during the time period of 2000–2001. The results show that the general efficiency across all English universities is very high; the average level of score is 93–95% across alternate models.

Thanassoulis et al. (2009) applied DEA to HEIs in England in the period of 2000–2001 to 2002–2003 to assess the cost structure and the performance of various HEI groups. They found that substantial gains of the order of 20–27% are feasible if all potential savings are directed at raising student numbers so that each HEI exploits to the full not only the operating and scale efficiency gains but also adjusts its student mix to maximise student numbers.

Studies on efficiency measurement of HEIs have also been extensively carried out in Australia. Avkiran (2001) used DEA to examine the relative efficiency of Australian universities. Three performance models are developed, namely, overall performance, performance on delivery of educational services and performance on fee-paying enrolments. The findings based on 1995 data showed that the university sector was performing well on technical and scale efficiency but there was room for improving performance on fee-paying enrolments. There were also small slacks in input utilisation. More universities were operating at decreasing returns to scale, indicating a potential to downsize. Abbott and Doucouliagos (2003) suggest that the Australian universities are operating at a fairly high level of efficiency relative to each other, although there is room for improvement in several universities.

There has been a growing literature on efficiency of HEIs in Asian countries in the recent period. Munisamy and Talib (2008) examined the efficiency of Malaysian public universities by conducting a benchmarking study using DEA. The results indicated a wide dispersion of efficiency amongst Malaysian public universities. The average efficiency score across the universities is about 60%, indicating a large scope for efficiency savings. The results also demonstrated that age plays a significant role in influencing the efficiency rating of universities.

Johnes and Yu (2008) examined the relative efficiency in the production of research of 109 Chinese regular universities in 2003 and 2004. Output variables measured the impact and productivity of research; input variables reflected staff, students, capital and resources. Mean efficiency is just over 90% when all input and output variables are included in the model, and this falls to just over 80% when student-related input variables are excluded from the model. Further investigation suggested that mean research efficiency is higher in comprehensive universities compared to specialist universities and in universities located in the coastal region compared to those in the western region of China.

Celik and Ecer (2009) measured the efficiency in accounting education in 45 public universities in Turkey using DEA. Their findings suggested that Turkish universities are successful in producing the most appropriate output and are usually using their input components in a favourable way. According to their model, accounting education delivered in the undergraduate programmes of the higher education system in Turkey is generally effective. But universities are using resources excessively to get the output. On the departmental basis, Turkish universities are technically effective to a greater extent.

In spite of growing research attention to efficiency of HEIs across the world, however, not many studies have been carried out in India, with an exception to a very recent study. Tyagi et al. (2009) evaluated the performance efficiencies of 19 academic departments of Indian Institute of Technology (IIT) Roorkee using the DEA technique. They have conducted an activity-based performance assessment of the departments by evaluating the efficiency of departments in teaching, placements and research. Their findings reveal that overall performance assessment is good for all science departments, while other departments need improvements in their activities.

The present study contributes to existing literature by examining technical and scale efficiency of higher technical education institutions in Kerala. We are not aware of previous attempts in this direction in the context of Kerala. We next proceed to outline the data and methodology used in the study.

8.4 Data and Input Output Specification

Data for examining efficiency have been obtained from a primary survey of a sample of engineering and polytechnic institutions in Kerala. Data for the period 2003–2004 through 2005–2006 were recorded from income and expenditure statement, balance sheet of the institutions and also the reports which these institutions reported to the All India Council for Technical Education (AICTE) as a mandatory disclosure. There are 86 engineering and 56 polytechnic institutions in Kerala. The engineering institutions fall into four broad types, namely, government (9), private aided (3), government-owned self-supported (23) and private unaided (50). In the case of polytechnic institutions, the type of institutions consists of government (44), private-aided (4) and the relatively new self-financing institutions (3).

From the above, a sample of 7 engineering (2 government, 2 private-aided, 2 government-owned self-supported and 1 private-unaided[2]) and 7 polytechnic (6 government and 1 aided) institutions are selected for the study. The size of the sample is rather small but quite representative of the government and aided institutions in the state. A brief profile of the institutions considered for the study for the most recent period is shown in Tables 8.1 and 8.2.

Having discussed the database, we proceed to describe the methodology used for efficiency analysis. A non-parametric method called the data envelopment analysis (DEA) is adopted for measuring the efficiency of HEIs. A 3-year panel data (2003–2004 through 2005–2006) is followed to estimate the efficiency of sample engineering and polytechnic institutions. A multistage DEA is used to estimate technical and scale efficiency scores of education institutions for the 3-year panel as well as cross-section data. This helps in identifying inefficiency of

[2] The unaided engineering institution which is included in the present study is regarded as one of the prominent private-unaided institutions in Kerala. Other private institutions that were approached were unwilling to provide data for the study, and, hence, the study is limited to only one private-unaided institution.

Table 8.1 Profile of engineering institutions 2005–2006

Institution code and year of establishment	Institution type	Student enrolment	Outturn of students	Teacher-student ratio
A (1991)	Government	781	247	1:15
B (1939)	Government	2,725	515	1:11
C (1960)	Private-aided	1,250	260	1:12
D (1961)	Private-aided	2,389	315	1:17
E (1989)	Government-owned self-supported	638	176	1:16
F (2003)	Government-owned self-supported	781	160	1:14
G (2001)	Private-unaided	1,055	196	1:7

Source: Primary Survey

Table 8.2 Profile of polytechnic institutions 2005–2006

Institution code and year of establishment	Institution type	Student enrolment	Outturn of students	Teacher-student ratio
A (1961)	Government	1,080	340	1:7
B (1958)	Government	780	257	1:10
C (1983)	Government	585	104	1:8
D (1994)	Government	240	28	1:5
E (1947)	Government	858	192	1:13
F (1962)	Government	441	90	1:6
G (1956)	Private-aided	363	121	1:8

Source: Primary Survey

institutions by analysing performance improvement potentials in this sector. The study assumes input-oriented approach, which implies that inputs are kept to a minimum while keeping output constant. The DEA model also involves a choice between constant returns to scale (CRS) and variable returns to scale (VRS). CRS assumes that there is no significant relationship between the scale of operation and efficiency. The DMUs are assumed to be operating at optimal scale of production. In reality, due to resource constraints and other issues, chances are that DMUs do not operate at optimal scale. Hence, assuming CRS would result in capturing technical efficiency scores with scale inefficiencies. In this context, Banker et al. (1984) adopted the VRS assumption, which means that the output produced by the DMUs will change in a disproportionate manner in response to input changes. In the present study, VRS is assumed and this yields estimates of technical as well as scale efficiency of DMUs. The discussion of specification of inputs and outputs is followed next.

The identification of input and output variables is a challenging task and has been done based on previous literature (Abbott and Doucouliagos (2003), Casu and Thanassoulis (2006), Johnes and Johnes (2005), Johnes (2006), Agasisti and Salerno(2007), Munisamy and Talib (2008), Thanassoulis et al. (2009)) and the

Table 8.3 Alternative definition of inputs and outputs

	Definition	Model 1	Model 2
Inputs			
Teaching_staff	Number of teaching staff in the institution	X	X
Nonteach_staff	Number of nonteaching staff employed in the institution	X	
Non-personnel_exp[a]	Non-personnel costs is the sum total of all the other costs which include expenditure on administration, office expenses, stationery, maintenance expenses, library, etc. It excludes personnel costs, that is, it does not include expenditure on salaries and allowances of teaching staff and wages and salaries of nonteaching staff		X
Output			
Students_enrol	Number of full-time equivalent students enrolled	X	X

[a]All the expenditure items are expressed in Indian Rupee. The physical inputs like number of teaching staff, nonteaching staff and the students enrolled are expressed in absolute numbers

availability of complete and consistent data set. Two models involving varying definitions of input are estimated. The definitions of inputs and outputs[3] used in the study as well as the models used to evaluate technical and scale efficiency of engineering and polytechnic institutions are shown in Table 8.3.

The output identified in both the models is full-time equivalent students enrolled in the HEI. Model 1 includes two physical inputs, namely, number of teaching staff and nonteaching staff; in model 2 teaching staff is expressed in numbers, while nonteaching staff is considered in terms of non-personnel expenditure rather than in physical units. The number of selected input and outputs for this efficiency study is confined to the rule of thumb of keeping the sum of input and output variables to be at least one-third of the sample size (Avkiran 2001). The descriptive statistics of inputs and outputs for each time period and for the 3 years put together are shown in Table 8.4.

The results of the DEA are obtained using DEAP (2.1) software developed by T. J. Coelli. The empirical estimates are discussed in the next section.

[3] The institutions included in the sample are engineering and polytechnic colleges which are affiliated to the respective universities. Very few education institutions other than universities or of deemed status offer postgraduate programme. Hence, our output measure for measuring efficiency is confined to number of students enrolled at the under graduation level.

Table 8.4 Descriptive statistics of inputs and outputs

Variables	No. of institutions	Minimum	Maximum	Mean	Standard deviation
Engineering	*2003–2004*				
Teaching_staff	7	47	248	117	70
Nonteach_staff	7	19	158	53	48
Non-personnel_exp	7	1,206,454	13,449,307	7,224,877	5,125,171
Students_enrol	7	580	2,598	1,243	700
Engineering	*2004–2005*				
Teaching_staff	7	51	250	121	69
Nonteach_staff	7	17	156	51	48
Non-personnel_exp	7	1,214,236	18,539,746	12,556,802	6,239,982
Students_enrol	7	588	2,606	1,263	712
Engineering	*2005–2006*				
Teaching_staff	7	52	253	125	70
Nonteach_staff	7	19	158	53	48
Non-personnel_exp	7	1,251,314	28,064,620	14,633,488	8,152,240
Students_enrol	7	638	2,725	1,328	758
Engineering	*3 × 7 = 21 observations*				
Teaching_staff	21	47	253	121	66
Nonteach_staff	21	13	158	51	45
Non-personnel_exp	21	1,206,454	28,064,620	11,471,722	7,051,424
Students_enrol	21	580	2,725	1,278	688
Polytechnics	*2003–2004*				
Teaching_staff	7	35	116	64	30
Nonteach_staff	7	16	170	59	55
Non-personnel_exp	7	102,150	1,987,484	541,296	646,767
Students_enrol	7	240	1,080	641	283
Polytechnics	*2004–2005*				
Teaching_staff	7	32	112	62	29
Nonteach_staff	7	15	165	56	54
Non-personnel_exp	7	201,844	1,425,714	527,224	415,240
Students_enrol	7	225	1,020	7	222
Polytechnics	*2005–2006*				
Teaching_staff	7	30	110	60	28
Nonteach_staff	7	16	160	54	52
Non-personnel_exp	7	199,984	1,687,412	603,372	528,641
Students_enrol	7	204	984	607	287
Polytechnics	*3 × 7 = 21 observations*				
Teaching_staff	21	30	116	62	28
Nonteach_staff	21	15	170	56	50
Non-personnel_exp	21	102,150	1,987,484	557,297	512,054
Students_enrol	21	377	1,080	678	210

8.5 Efficiency of Engineering and Polytechnic Institutions in Kerala: Empirical Analysis

8.5.1 Technical and Scale Efficiency Scores

Technical and scale efficiency scores for the sample of engineering and polytechnic institutions in Kerala for each year and also for the 3 years taken together are computed and shown in Table 8.5.

The mean technical efficiency for the entire period (2003–2004 to 2005–2006) for engineering institutions is 88 and 84%, respectively, for model 1 and model 2. The scale efficiency scores of engineering institutions do not differ much across the models and is 84 and 83%, respectively. Similarly, the mean efficiency scores of polytechnic institutions for the panel data show technical (scale) efficiency score of 92 and 93% (78 and 82%) across the models.

The table also shows the efficiency scores for engineering and polytechnic institutions for each year. When the inputs are taken in physical terms (model 1), it may be noted that the mean technical and scale efficiency scores of engineering institutions ranges from 89 to 92% and 86 to 93%, respectively, for the 3 years. When monetary value is used in place of number of nonteaching staff (model 2), the average technical efficiency scores lie in the range of 81 and 84%, indicating relatively lower level of technical efficiency. The scale efficiency estimates vary from 85 to 90% which is also lower than those obtained from model 1.

The technical and scale efficiency scores for polytechnic institutions for the panel period range between 91–92% and 78–82%, respectively. The results obtained from model 1 in the case of polytechnic institutions show the technical and scale efficiency scores range between 90–92% and 78–85%, respectively. However, model 2 results show better technical efficiency scores in the case of polytechnic institutions. In sum, our estimates indicate that the polytechnic institutions are relatively more technically efficient, while there is higher scale efficiency in engineering institutions in Kerala. It should be noted that the technical efficiency of engineering and polytechnic institutions have remained reasonably stable over the three years and is in general higher than scale efficiency except in model 2 for 2004–2005 and 2005–2006. The difference between technical and scale efficiency scores is especially large in the case of polytechnic institutions.

To test the robustness and stability amongst the models, Spearman's correlation between the efficiency scores from the two models is calculated and shown in Table 8.6. The correlation coefficients are 0.81 (engineering) and 0.85 (polytechnics), suggesting that there are rather small differences in the efficiency ranking between the two models.

It may be noted from the table that the rank correlation coefficients between the efficiencies of corresponding models are all highly significant and exceed 0.80. The higher values of the coefficient indicate that results are robust for these models.

DEA has also been used to identify the returns to scale in which DMU operates and also to find out the peers for each DMU. The results shown in Table 8.7 and for

Table 8.5 Mean technical and scale efficiency scores of engineering and polytechnic institutions in Kerala

Time period	Engineering				Polytechnics			
	Model 1		Model 2		Model 1		Model 2	
	Technical efficiency	Scale efficiency	Technical efficiency	Scale efficiency	Technical efficiency	Scale efficiency	Technical efficiency	Scale efficiency
2003–2004	0.917	0.861	0.836	0.828	0.907	0.851	0.930	0.853
2004–2005	0.895	0.898	0.824	0.864	0.921	0.837	0.922	0.844
2005–2006	0.906	0.933	0.814	0.903	0.913	0.787	0.960	0.911
2003–2004 to 2005–2006 (all)	0.884	0.840	0.836	0.828	0.915	0.783	0.926	0.822

Source: Computations based on primary data
Note: Models 1 and 2 as shown in Table 8.3

Table 8.6 Spearman's correlation coefficient amongst the two DEA models (engineering and polytechnics), 2005–2006

	Engineering		Polytechnics	
	Model 1	Model 2	Model 1	Model 2
Model 1	1		1	
Model 2	0.81	1	0.85	1

Source: Authors' computations using primary data

Table 8.7 Efficiency scores and returns to scale of engineering institutions in Kerala, 2005–2006

Firm	Technical efficiency	Scale efficiency	RTS	Peers	Peer counts
Government (A)	1	1	MPSS	A	4
Government (B)	1	0.713	DRS	B	0
Aided (C)	1	0.907	DRS	C	2
Aided (D)	0.637	0.930	DRS	C,A	0
GOVTSS (E)	0.658	0.812	IRS	A	0
GOVTSS (F)	0.852	1	MPSS	A	0
Unaided (G)	0.548	0.958	DRS	C,A	0
Mean	0.814	0.903			

Source: Authors' computations using primary data
Note: *RTS*, *IRS*, *DRS* and *MPSS* denote returns to scale, increasing returns to scale and decreasing returns to scale and most productive scale size, respectively. *GOVTSS* means government-owned self-supported institution

engineering and polytechnic institutions are based on model 2 which has the appeal that it incorporates inputs measured in physical units and monetary units. In any case, the difference in efficiency scores across the two models is rather small.

It can be noted from Table 8.7 that on an average, engineering institutions in the sample are 81 and 90% technical and scale efficient, respectively. When the scores of each institution is examined, it is seen that only one government institution (A) is both technical and scale efficient in the sample. All the government institutions and an aided institution (C) are technical efficient. The results clearly indicate the unaided institution (G) is the least technical efficient (55%) institution in the sample. However, the scale efficiency score of this unaided institution (96%) shows that the institution is close to optimum scale of operation.

The returns to scale for the institutions shows that most of the relatively inefficient institutions are operating under decreasing returns to scale, with an exception of a relatively inefficient government-owned self-supported institution (E), which is operating in increasing returns to scale. This implies that institution E has scope for expanding its operation and reaping benefits of scale. It is interesting to compare the scale of operations of these institutions in terms of their size, measured by student enrolment. That is, institutions (B, C and D) operating under decreasing returns to scale are found to be large-sized ones indicating that they have exhausted scale

Table 8.8 Efficiency scores and returns to scale of polytechnic institutions in Kerala, 2005–2006

Firm	Technical efficiency	Scale efficiency	Returns to scale	Peers	Peer counts
Government (A)	1	0.633	DRS	A	0
Government (B)	1	0.833	DRS	B	1
Government (C)	1	1	MPSS	C	0
Government (D)	1	1	MPSS	D	1
Government (E)	1	0.981	IRS	E	0
Government (F)	1	1	MPSS	F	1
Private aided (G)	0.717	0.927	DRS	B,FD	0
Mean	0.960	0.911			

Source: Authors' computations using primary data
Note: Same as in Table 8.7

economies. A similar exercise is done for polytechnic institutions, and the results are shown in Table 8.8.

Table 8.8 shows that the mean technical and scale efficiency scores of polytechnic institutions are 96 and 91%, indicating higher efficiency of polytechnics compared to engineering institutions in Kerala. The examination of individual institution shows that three government institutions are technical and scale efficient across the group. The table also indicates that six out of seven institutions in the sample are technical efficient. The examination of the returns to scale for each institution reveals that most of the inefficient institutions are operating under decreasing returns to scale with the exception of institution E which is under the increasing returns to scale. Interestingly, institutions A, B, and E are relatively large-sized ones, and all these institutions except E are experiencing increasing returns to scale, thus pointing out that they have scope for reaping scale economies.

In order to compare the technical and scale efficiency scores between the engineering and polytechnic institutions, radar charts are plotted. Radar charts or spider charts are used to examine the relative values for a single datapoint and to locate similar points or dissimilar points. Radars representing technical and scale efficiency scores of engineering and polytechnic institutions for the period 2006–2007 are shown in Figs. 8.1 and 8.2, respectively.

The radars clearly depict the higher technical efficiency of polytechnics over engineering institutions, while the converse is true for scale efficiency.

8.6 Summary and Conclusion

This chapter has provided an overview of efficiency of technical education institutions in Kerala, India. The chapter uses a non-parametric approach, namely, DEA to investigate the efficiency (technical and scale) of engineering and polytechnic institutions for the time period 2005–2006. The study is based on the primary data collected through institutional survey of seven engineering and seven polytechnic institutions in Kerala. The efficiency scores of these institutions are computed and

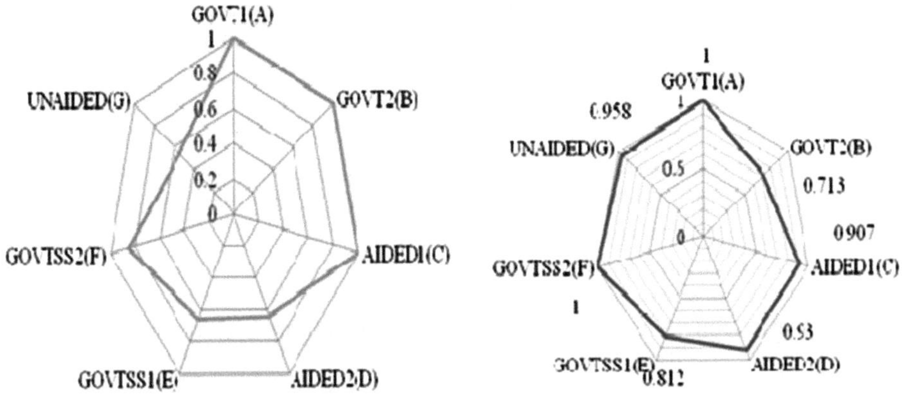

Fig. 8.1 Technical and scale efficiency scores of engineering institutions in Kerala in 2005–2006 (Source: Same as that in Table 8.7)

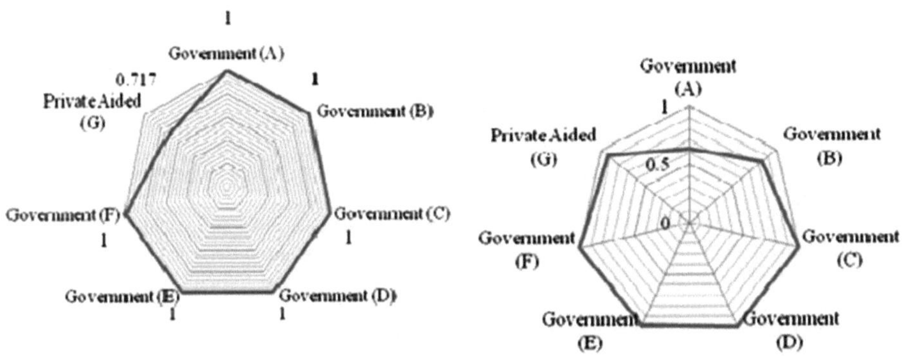

Fig. 8.2 Technical and scale efficiency scores of polytechnic institutions in Kerala in 2005–2006 (Source: Same as that in Table 8.8)

compared, and a simple exercise in benchmarking is attempted by employing a non-parametric approach (DEA).

An input-oriented multistage DEA analysis is carried out for technical and scale efficiency scores. The mean score of technical efficiency of all engineering institutions across the two models varies from 0.81 to 0.92. The two models are distinguished on the basis of choice of input variables. When the technical efficiency scores are compared across the types of institutions, it is to be noted that a government institution is found technical as well as scale efficient in CRS and VRS assumptions in both the models. The scale efficiency ranges between 0.83 and 0.90 across the models. Scale efficiency also throws light on the returns to scale, and it shows that government and aided institutions operate under decreasing returns to scale. The study also shows that relatively inefficient institutions including aided, government-owned self-supported and the unaided institutions operate on increasing returns to scale, indicating scope for expansion of activities in these institutions. The mean score of technical efficiency of the polytechnic institutions across the models ranges from 0.91 to 0.96, indicating better technical efficiency in polytechnics in Kerala. The average scale efficiency of polytechnic institutions is in the range from 0.78 to 0.91 across the models and is lower when compared to engineering institutions. The study has also found that all the large-sized engineering degree and diploma institutions with an exception of one polytechnic institution (E) have exhausted scale economies and are operating under decreasing returns to scale.

Thus, overall the government institutions in the sample score over the other types of institutions in terms of technical efficiency. These institutions appear to use resources efficiently, thus justifying the public expenditure incurred on them.

Acknowledgements This chapter is extracted from the Ph.D. thesis of the first author. It was presented earlier in a seminar at the Department of Humanities and Social Sciences, IIT Madras. We acknowledge the comments received from an examiner of the thesis. We take responsibility for errors, if any, in the chapter.

References

Abbott M, Doucouliagos C (2003) The efficiency of Australian universities: a data envelopment analysis. Econ Edu Rev 22(1):89–97

Agasisti T, Salerno C (2007) Assessing the cost efficiency of Italian universities. Edu Econ 15(4):455–471

Athanassapoulos AD, Shale E (1997) Assessing the comparative efficiency of higher education institutions in the U.K by means of data envelopment analysis. Educ Econ 5:117–134

Avkiran NK (2001) Investigating technical and scale efficiencies of Australian Universities through data envelopment analysis. Socioecon Plann Sci 35:57–80

Banker RD, Charnes A, Cooper WW (1984) Some models for estimating technical and scale inefficiencies in data envelopment analysis. Manag Sci 30:1078–1092

Casu B, Thanassoulis E (2006) Evaluating cost efficiency in central administrative services in UK universities. Omega, Elsevier 34(5):417–426

Celik O, Ecer A (2009) Efficiency in accounting education: evidence from Turkish universities. Crit Perspect Acc 20:614–634

Charnes A, Cooper WW, Rhodes E (1978) Measuring the efficiency of decision making units. Eur J Oper Res 2:429–444

Farrell MJ (1957) The measurement of productive efficiency. J R Stat Soc 120(3):253–290

Johnes J (2006) Data envelopment analysis and its application to the measurement of efficiency in higher education. Econ Edu Rev 25(3):273–288

Johnes G, Johnes J (2005) Higher education institutions' costs and efficiency: taking the decomposition a further step. Lancaster University working paper no: 003052

Johnes J, Yu L (2008) Measuring the research performance of Chinese higher education institutions using data envelopment analysis. China Econ Rev 19:679–696

Munisamy S, Talib AM (2008) Benchmarking the efficiency of Malaysian Public Universities via data envelopment analysis. In: Proceedings of the 8th international business research conference, Dubai, UAE, pp 1–12

Salerno C (2003) What we know about the efficiency of higher education institutions: the best evidence. A report for the Center for Higher Education Policy Studies, University of Twente

Thanassoulis E et al (2009) Cost and efficiency of higher education institutions in England: a DEA analysis. Lancaster University Management School, Working paper 008

Tilak JBG (2001) Higher education and development in Kerala, Working paper no.5, Centre for Socio- Economic and Environmental Studies, Kerala
Tyagi P, Yadav SP, Singh SP (2009) Relative performance of academic departments using DEA with sensitivity analysis. Eval Program Plann 32:168–177
Worthington CA (2001) An empirical survey of frontier efficiency measurement techniques in education. Edu Econ 9(3):245–268

Author Index

A
Abbott, M., 132, 134
Adams, R., 80–82, 87
Adelman, I., 79
Agasisti, T., 134
Agenor, P., 40
Ahluwalia, I.J., 57
Allen, R.G.D., 60
Alvan, A., 4
Anoopkumar, M., 120
Arnold, J., 25
Athanassapoulos, A.D., 131
Audretsch D.B., 15
Avkiran, N.K., 132, 135
Aw, B.Y., 25

B
Balaramaiah, T., 110
Balasubrahmanya, M.H., 61, 62
Baltagi, B.H., 15
Banker, R.D., 129, 134
Bardhan, P.K., 110, 114
Barik, K., 58
Barnett, A.H., 60
Barro, R.J., 2
Bartel, A., 24
Bartelsman, E., 23
Basu, A.K., 101, 102, 108, 111, 113
Batra, G., 23, 25
Becker, G.S., 25
Berg, E., 114
Bernstein, I., 101
Besley, T., 101
Bhalotra, S., 114
Bhende, M.J., 110
Binswanger, H.P., 110
Biswas, A., 40
Blalock, G., 25
Blaug, M., 101
Bouhga-Hagbe, J., 82
Broadman, H.G., 4
Brynjolfsson, E., 4
Buckley, P.J., 14
Buongiorno, J., 60

C
Caloghiro Y., 60
Cameron, T., 60
Campos, R., 81
Card, D., 110
Casu, B., 134
Caves, R.E., 13
Celik, O., 132
Chami, R., 80
Chand, S., 23
Chang, K., 60
Charnes, A., 129, 130, 134
Chau, N., 102
Chaudhuri, S., 59
Choi, K., 12
Christensen, L.R., 60
Ciccone, A., 4, 12
Cline, W., 56
Coate, S., 101
Cohen, M., 62
Cooper, W.W., 129, 130, 134

D
Das, D., 59
Das, S., 102, 108, 111, 113
Dasgupta, P., 114

N.S. Siddharthan and K. Narayanan (eds.), *Human Capital and Development: The Indian Experience*, DOI 10.1007/978-81-322-0857-0,

Datt, G., 110
Davidson, O., 56
de Palomo, L., 81
Dearden, L., 23, 25
Denison, E.F., 60
Denny, M., 60
Dessing, M., 114
Devarajan, S., 25
Docquier, F., 79
Doctor, M., 4, 13
Doherty, V.S., 110
Dollar, D., 25
Doms, M., 23
Doonan, J., 61
Doucouliagos, C., 132, 134
Dowlatabadi, H., 56
Drèze, J., 101
Duraisamy, M., 26
Durand, J., 79
Dutta, B., 102, 108, 111, 113

E
Easterly, W., 23, 55
Ecer, A., 132
Edmonds, J., 56
Ekanayake, E.M., 80
El-Hamidi, F., 114
Epifani, P., 12

F
Faini, R., 79
Fankhauser, S., 56
Feliciano, Z.M., 12
Felipe, J., 60
Fernandes, A.M., 23
Forre, E.S., 4, 12
Foulon, J., 62
Frank, R., 82
Fraumeni, B.M., 60
Fujita, M., 15
Fullenkamp, C., 80
Fuss, M., 60

G
Gancia, G., 12
Ganguli, I., 60
Gao, T., 13
Gertler, P., 25
Ghosh, B.N., 4
Ghosh, S., 40
Gibson, J., 61, 64
Glaeser, E., 2
Goldar, B.N., 23, 40, 58, 64, 71, 114
Goldberg, P., 40
Gollop, F.M., 60
Griliches, Z., 25
Grossman, G.M., 11
Grubb, M., 56
Guha-Khasnobis, B., 40

H
Halkides, M., 80
Hallward-Driemeier, M., 25
Hari, K.S., 92
Harrison, R., 12
Harriss, R.G., 23
Hellerstein, J., 24
Helpman, E., 11
Hildebrandt, N., 79
Hitt, L.M., 4
Hogan, W., 60
Horowitz, A., 3
Hseu, J.S., 61
Hudson, E.A., 60

I
Ilmakunnas, P., 23, 25
Ince, P.J., 60
Isaksson, A., 23
Isgut, A.E., 23
Ismail, R., 13

J
Jahjah, S., 80
Javorcik, B., 25
Jha, R., 60
Johnes, G., 131, 134
Johnes, J., 131, 132, 134
Jones, P., 23, 25
Jorgenson, D.W., 60
Jung, J.H., 12

K
Kalita, G., 59
Kanbur, R., 40, 101
Kannan, K.P., 92
Karlan, D., 3
Kathuria, V., 14, 23–25, 27, 30, 33

Kato, A., 49
Kee, K.L., 25
Kesselman, J.R., 101
Khera, R., 101
Kim, K.S., 4, 12
Kiso, J., 40
Kokko, A., 14
Kraay, A., 25
Krueger, A.B., 41, 110
Krugman, P.R., 14, 25
Kshirsagar, K.G., 110
Kumar, A., 64
Kumari, A., 23, 40

L
Lal, K., 13
Lall, S., 4
Lanjouw, P., 3
Lanoie, P., 61, 62
Laplante, B., 61, 62
Lashof, D., 56
Lau, L.J., 60
Lehmann, E.E., 15
Levine, R., 23, 55
Levinsohn, J., 24, 27
Lewis, W.A., 114
Li, X., 60
Lichtenberg, F., 24
Licona, G.H., 114
Lindahl, M., 41
Lipton, M., 101
Liu, Z., 14, 17
Lopez Cordova, J.E., 81
Lopez-Acevedo, G., 24, 25

M
Ma, H., 61, 64
Mahambare, V., 121
Mahmud, S., 60
Maiti, D., 12, 40, 42
Maiti, S., 40, 42
Majumdar, R., 27
Malamud, O., 3
Maliranta, M., 23, 25
Mankiw, N.G., 11
Manning, A., 110
Marjit, S., 40
Massey, D.S., 79
Mathur, L., 102
Mazumdar, D., 26
McCormick, B., 80
McKenzie, D., 79
Mehrotra, S., 102, 103
Melitz, M.J., 25
Mellor, J.W., 114
Mengistae, T., 25
Mincer, J., 24
Mitra, A., 12, 40, 49, 50
Mitra, D., 23, 25
Mongia, P., 57–59
Mookherjee, D., 43
Mora, J., 82
Mourelatos, A., 60
Mukherjee, D., 24, 26
Mukherji, A., 110
Munisamy, S., 132, 134
Murgai, R., 3
Murty, M.N., 60

N
Nadi, S., 40
Nadkarni, R., 121
Nagaraj, R., 59
Nair, K.N., 120
Napel, S., 43
Narayanan, K., 64, 71
Nardinelli, C., 2
Neumark, D., 24
Newhouse, D., 3
Nicita, A., 28, 32
Nielsen, H., 23
Noorbakhsh, F., 4, 13

O
Obstfeld, M., 25
Okada, A., 15
Olarreaga, M., 28, 32
Oxley, L., 61, 64

P
Page, J., 81, 87
Paloni, A., 4, 13
Pandit, B.L., 12
Pant, B., 79
Papaioannou, E., 4, 11
Parrado, E.A., 79
Parson, E.A., 56
Paul, S., 60
Pavnik, N., 40
Petrin, A., 24, 27
Pradhan, G., 58

R
Raj, R.S.N., 25–27, 33
Rajan, R.G., 82
Rajesh, S.N.R., 24, 27, 30
Raju, P.S.S., 110
Rao, B.B., 60
Rao, V.B., 110
Rapoport, H., 79
Ratha, D., 80
Ravallion, M., 101
Ravi, K., 102
Ravindranath, N.H., 56
Ray, D., 43, 108
Ray, S., 13
Reed, H., 23, 25
Reutter, K., 6o
Rhodes, E., 129, 130
Richels, R., 56
Roberts, M.J., 25
Rodriguez, E.R., 82
Rodrik, D., 25
Romer, D., 11
Romer, P.M., 2, 11
Rosenthal, S.S., 15
Rosholm, M., 23
Rotmans, J., 56
Round, J., 40
Roy, J., 56, 58, 60
Rudra, A., 110

S
Sahu, S.K., 64, 71
Salerno, C., 129, 134
Salvanes, K.G., 4, 12
Sanstad, A., 58
Sarkar, S., 26, 56
Sathaye, J.A., 56–59
Scheinkman, J., 2
Schenzler, C., 3
Schultz, T.W., 25
Schumacher, K., 58, 59
Schwartz, S.L., 6o
Sen, A., 101
Sen, K., 23–25, 27, 30, 33
Shale, E., 131
Shang, J.K., 61
Shleifer, A., 2
Shukla, P.R., 56
Siddharthan, N.S., 1, 4, 12, 13, 15
Simon, C.J., 2
Singh, S.P., 133
Solow, R.M., 60
Spatafora, N., 80
Sreedharan, T.P., 120
Strange, W.C., 15
Subramanyam, A., 82
Sun, X., 4
Suryadarma, D., 3

T
Takayama, A., 60
Takii, S., 23, 25
Talib, A.M., 132, 134
Tan, H., 23–25
Tansini, R., 14
Taylor, J.E., 79, 82
Thanassoulis, E., 132, 134
Thompson, H., 6o
Tilak, J.B.G., 127
Tiongson, E.R., 82
Tirpak, D., 56
Tol, R.S.J., 56
Tyagi, P., 133
Tybout, J., 23

U
Uma, R., 59
Unni, J., 59

V
Vainionmaki, J., 23, 25
Valdivia, M., 3
Van Reenen, J., 23, 25
Varian, H.R., 60
Venables, A.J., 14
Von Braun, J., 101

W
Wadhwa, D., 59
Wagner, J., 25
Wahba, J., 80
Wallsten, S., 25
Waverman, L., 60
Wei, Y., 2
Weil, D.N., 11
Weyant, J., 56
Williams, C.C., 40
Winston, T., 25
Woodruff, C., 79

Wooldridge, J., 33
Worthington, C.A., 129

X
Xu, C., 25

Y
Yadav, S.P., 133
Yang, D., 79, 81
Yeaple, S.R., 4, 13
Yi, F., 60
Youssef, A., 4, 13
Yu, L., 132
Yussof, I., 13

Z
Zejan, M.C., 14
Zenteno, R., 79

Subject Index

A
Acquisition, 6
ADF. *See* Augmented Dickey-Fuller(ADF)
Agglomeration, 5, 15, 16, 20, 21
Agricultural productivity, 7, 102, 103, 107, 108, 110, 115, 118, 120, 122–124
Annual Survey of industries, 16, 28, 51, 59, 63
Augmented Dickey-Fuller(ADF), 97–99

B
BSE, 65, 67, 68, 71, 73, 74

C
Capital stock, 2, 11, 16, 17, 21, 28
Carbon dioxide (CO_2), 55, 56
Causality, 2, 14, 90, 91, 93–95
Central statistical organization, 52
Centre for monitoring Indian economy (CMIE), 29, 57, 64–73
Climate change, 55, 56
CMIE. *See* Centre for monitoring Indian economy (CMIE)
Competitiveness, 1, 13, 15, 25, 74, 102, 104, 109, 110
Complementarity, 57, 64
Consumption, 6, 8, 40, 56, 63, 65, 67, 74, 79–82, 86, 90–95, 97–99

D
Data envelopment analysis (DEA), 128–135, 137, 139–141
Decision-making units (DMUs), 129–131, 134
Demand, 1, 2, 8, 12, 39, 40, 44, 51, 55, 56, 60, 61, 63, 79, 96, 102–104, 107–110, 112, 113, 115, 120–121
Demographic, 1
Development expenditure, 6, 43, 51–53
Dividend, 1
DMEs, 35
Dummy variable, 26, 52, 65, 73

E
Efficiency, 5, 7, 13, 18, 19, 25–27, 56, 58, 61, 63, 72–74, 96, 102, 127–142
EGS. *See* Employment guarantee scheme (EGS)
Emerging, 1, 5, 20, 21, 40, 58, 62, 77, 83
Employment guarantee scheme (EGS), 101, 102, 114
Endogenous(eity), 2, 27, 32–35, 60, 82
Energy intensity, 6, 55–74
Enrolment, 1, 5, 7, 12, 15–17, 20, 21, 51, 52, 127, 132, 134, 139
Enterprise, 6, 39, 40, 51, 61, 74, 81
Exogenous, 2
Export, 6–8, 14–17, 20, 25, 26, 28, 29, 40, 62, 74, 80

F
FDI. *See* Foreign direct investment (FDI)
Financial, 7, 35, 61, 79–81, 86, 94, 127
Foreign direct investment (FDI), 4–5, 12–20, 62, 80, 81, 98, 99
Foreign exchange, 82
Formal sector, 6, 12, 26, 28, 30, 33–35, 39–41, 43, 44, 49, 52

N.S. Siddharthan and K. Narayanan (eds.), *Human Capital and Development: The Indian Experience*, DOI 10.1007/978-81-322-0857-0, © Springer India 2013

G
GDP, 15, 56, 79–81, 83, 86, 88–90, 95, 97–99
Generalised least squares, 18
GFCF. *See* Gross fixed capital formation (GFCF)
Gini coefficient, 52, 81, 89
Granger Causality, 78, 90, 91, 93–95
Greenhouse gas, 55
Gross enrolment ratio, 1, 16, 17, 127
Gross fixed capital formation (GFCF), 90–92, 94, 97–99
Gross value added (GVA), 28
Growth rate, 6, 12, 13, 20, 29, 31, 43, 56, 58, 59, 63, 69
GVA. *See* Gross value added (GVA)

H
Health, 2, 5–7, 14, 16, 17, 20, 21, 24, 53, 78, 79, 103, 127
HEIs. *See* Higher Education Institutions (HEIs)
Herfindahl-Hirschman index(HHI), 26, 28, 29, 32–34
Higher Education Institutions (HEIs), 128–129, 131–133
Higher-secondary education, 21

I
IAMs. *See* Integrated assessment models (IAMs)
Import, 6, 26, 28, 29, 49, 63, 65, 72–74
Income, 3, 7, 8, 11, 16, 20, 21, 40, 41, 51, 79–82, 88–95, 97–99, 101, 102, 104, 106, 110–118, 121, 123, 133
Indian manufacturing, 6, 24, 26, 29, 34, 57, 63, 64, 74
Indian migrants, 83
Industrial agglomeration, 5, 21
Inequalities, 6, 12, 40, 41, 51, 53, 81, 86, 89, 90
Informalisation, 6
Informal sector, 6, 24, 26, 27, 30, 31, 33–35, 39–53
Infrastructure, 5, 6, 21, 24, 25, 41, 53, 63, 101
Innovation, 4, 11
Integrated assessment models (IAMs), 56

K
KLEM, 59

L
Labour intensity, 6, 55–74
Labour productivity, 2, 5, 6, 11–21, 49, 55, 58, 61
Land, 3, 33, 103, 107–110, 112–114, 117–119, 123
Liberalized, 3, 12, 40, 49, 58
Low-income, 2, 40, 95
Low-skilled, 5, 6, 26

M
Manufacturing, 4, 6, 8, 12, 16, 17, 23–35, 40, 41, 45–49, 51, 57–60, 62–64, 74, 81
Market structure, 23, 102, 110
Micro-credit, 3
Micro-entrepreneurs, 3
Middle-income, 2, 95
MOSPI, 63
Multi-skilled, 4

N
National Rural Employment Guarantee Act (NREGA), 7, 8, 101–124
National Sample Survey Organisation (NSSO), 27, 43, 44, 51
NDMEs, 35
Neoclassical, 2
Net state domestic product (NSDP), 51, 52, 92–94, 97
Non-resident, 7, 8, 77
Non-resident Indians (NRIs), 77, 84, 86, 88
NREGA. *See* National Rural Employment Guarantee Act (NREGA)
NSDP. *See* Net state domestic product (NSDP)
NSSO. *See* National Sample Survey Organisation (NSSO)

O
OAMEs, 35

P
Panel data, 15, 50, 71, 73, 80, 133, 137
Pollution, 6, 8, 61, 62
Poor, 3, 7, 14, 40, 41, 63, 78, 81, 89, 92, 95, 101–104, 106–123

Population, 3, 5, 8, 11, 13–17, 20, 21, 40, 43, 44, 52, 56, 78, 83, 84, 89, 90, 102, 110
Poverty ratio, 52, 86, 89–93, 95, 97
Private aided, 128, 133, 134, 140
PROWESS database, 29
Pulp and paper industries, 6, 55–74

R
Randomised, 3, 49, 71–73
RBI. *See* Reserve bank of India (RBI)
Remittances, 7, 8, 77–99
Research and development, 23, 24, 73
Reserve bank of India (RBI), 29, 77, 84, 86, 88
Returns to sale, 2, 11, 61, 129, 132, 134, 137, 139–142

S
Savings, 6, 58, 74, 80, 110, 111, 123, 132
Self-employed, 3, 4, 80, 120, 121
Service-oriented, 3, 4
Simultaneity bias, 24, 27
Skill-labour, 4
Socio-economic, 1
Stationarity, 90, 97–99
Stochastic frontier, 44, 52, 129
Substitution, 6, 16, 20, 56, 57, 59–62, 64, 74, 110, 113
Supply-push, 39, 41, 49–53

T
Target income, 102, 111–118, 123
Technical and scale efficiency, 137–140
Technical and vocational education and training (TVET), 3
Technical education, 5, 8, 52, 127–142
Total factor productivity growth (TFPG), 24, 26, 27, 29–35, 58
Trade openness, 23
TVET. *See* Technical and vocational education and training (TVET)

U
UNFCCC, 55
Unorganised, 7, 8, 26, 40, 51, 53, 59
Unskilled, 5, 103, 105
Urbanisation, 5, 14–17, 20, 21

V
Vocational institutes, 51
Vulnerability, 39–53, 104

W
Wage, 3, 6, 12, 13, 18, 19, 26, 40, 49–53, 58, 59, 63–65, 102–110, 112–118, 120, 121, 123, 124, 135
Wholesale price index (WPI), 17, 28, 29

MIX
Papier aus verantwortungsvollen Quellen
Paper from responsible sources
FSC® C105338

If you have any concerns about our products,
you can contact us on
ProductSafety@springernature.com

In case Publisher is established outside the EU,
the EU authorized representative is:
Springer Nature Customer Service Center GmbH
Europaplatz 3, 69115 Heidelberg, Germany

Printed by Libri Plureos GmbH
in Hamburg, Germany